PEOPLE OF THE MIRROR

People
of the
Mirror

An Intimate Look at Loneliness

Dr. RICHARD PRICE

NEW HORIZON PRESS

FAR HILLS, NEW JERSEY
Distributed by Scribner Book Companies

Library of Congress Cataloging-in-Publication Data

Price, Richard H.
    People of the mirror

    Bibliography: p.
    1. Loneliness. 2. Interpersonal relations. I. Title.
BF575.L7P75   1985   158'.2   85-29730
ISBN 0-88282-015-X
Manufactured in the United States of America

Table of Contents

ACKNOWLEDGMENTS

I am indebted to the many supportive people who added their critical comments, suggestions and balancing humor to my efforts in producing this book. My deep appreciation to Van Richards, Jan Moosbruker, Morrie Schwartz, Shaun McNiff, Barbara Schwartz, Roy Fairfield, Diane Raintree and Joan Dunphy.

And of course, a special thanks to Jean Price, Marguerite Whittley May, Geraldine Naidus and Jo-Ann Caratelli, who were with me all the way. For this and your love—thank you.

I hope that I have done justice to the "people of the mirror"—friends, clients, neighbors and others like them from around the country that I have written about here.

I thank them all for willingly sharing their personal lives with me as a part of this project. I have gained so much from them that my expression of affection seems very inadequate.

Richard Price

Boxford, Massachusetts

PREFACE

"Human beings awake to consciousness to find themselves in
chaos. They then try to impose order
on this chaos in order to make life
endurable. . . We cannot verify
whether the chart that we make of
the mysterious universe corre-
sponds to elusive reality; but in
order to live, we have to make this
chart, realizing it is an act of faith
which is also an act of self-preserva-
tion."

Arnold Toynbee

In many ways I view this book as a guidebook for anyone
who experiences loneliness as a problem and would like to
do something about it. I recognize some risks to the guidebook approach which I would like to share with you. For
one thing, I choose to avoid any authoritative "how to" or
"paint by numbers" presentation which in any suggests
that if you simply follow my lead, you will get where you
want to go. For me to do this would be to disrespect you.
But this book is the closest I can come to being a potential
sounding board and resource for your own investigation.

Many years ago, I was the navigator/second officer of a
cargo-passenger ship, sailing in the South Pacific. I remember a time, one particularly glorious evening, just
after dusk, when I had completed taking my sextant sights
of the stars and had laid down a carefully worked-out plot
on the chart, indicating the ship's position. I was jubilant
about the accuracy of my navigational calculations, and
was about to report them to the captain, when he popped
into the chartroom. "Well, Captain," I announced, trying
not to look too pleased with myself but pointing decisively

to my fix on the chart, "We are right here!" No answer. In the dead silence following my statement, I could sense the old captain not looking at the chart at all. I felt as though he squared his shoulders and loomed taller as the seconds ticked by. Finally, he smiled and looking me squarely in the eye, he said in his deep Norwegian accent, "Mr. Price, remember dis words, 'Dot is var you tink ve are!!' "

It was one of the great lessons of my life—reality is such a subjective thing. There just isn't any concrete, exact pinpointing of truth that is completely relevant for all of us. I was an experienced navigator, but my observations were only my assessment of truth, my truth—not his, not yours.

These recollections relate to our way of examining loneliness. There are few givens and no "experts" who have final answers. We all have to rely on ourselves, because no one else can really presume the ability to define our own inner experiences. Besides, when we can allow ourselves to be honest, nobody knows us better than we do ourselves.

I came to this writing naturally, out of a need to clarify things for myself, to put into some order my own understanding of loneliness. Experience tells me not to underrate the potential of what you and I have in common. We each come with our own brand of expertise. I can share my observations and experiences, and if, through this presentation, something that I say has meaning for you or enhances something you are feeling, then this effort will have served its purpose.

Although I am a psychotherapist and educator, I believe in "self-help." I feel that the concepts of "self-help" are the key to the usefulness of this book, and for anyone who is lonely, whoever she or he may be. By "self-help" I do not mean that we have to go it strictly alone. Whether we like it or not, we are always connected to others in some way, no matter how isolated we may feel. When we help ourselves we draw upon inner resources and relationships established over a lifetime of experience; all that we have seen and felt, heard or read about, people we have met or seen, things that we have done or had done to us. However, despite our resources, sometimes we feel helpless and alone.

Problems of loneliness can never be totally solved, yet most people seek situational answers that they can use to solve immediate problems. The two questions that I hear the most are, *"What do you do and other people do when they are lonely?"* and, *"How can I learn to manage my own loneliness?"* During the years that I have been involved in studying the experience of loneliness, I have found very little previous research dealing with these emotionally-charged questions. I want to do that now.

My empathy is with people who experience painful emotions, people who are lonely now or view loneliness as a problem in their lives. I would like them to discover that their feelings need not be as crippling as they may believe—that is the goal of this book.

My interest, then, is in presenting some of my own understanding of the experience as it has touched my life and the lives of people I have known and worked with. The focus of this work is mainly on psychological aspects of loneliness. It is not intended as a definitive study of the subject, but is rather a pointed selection of observations and ideas about certain facets of the loneliness experience which I believe have particular, if not crucial, bearing on how we live and deal with loneliness.

Many people agreed to become a part of this study. As it is their lives and feelings rather than names which are important to me, I have given them pseudonyms here, juxtaposed events, and disguised other data where appropriate in order to respect their privacy. However, the words spoken and the essential facts have been accurately reported.

Two broad and interwoven topics run through this book. The one I call *understanding* looks at a number of myths and current notions about loneliness and sets the scene for our exploration. It is the psychological setting in which I believe most of us live our lives. I have attempted to present you with a varied number of emotional and thoughtful portraits of this experience we label "loneliness"—what it is or is not, how it develops, how we and others feel and react to it.

The second topic I call *managing*. It includes looking at some of the features of loneliness which I feel remain present through all its variations. From this exploration I have ventured to develop some alternative ways of perceiving the loneliness experience and making personal changes to deal with it, if change is warranted.

At the end of the book I have listed a number of other books, articles and studies which have been of special value to me, either as direct resources or simply as a joy to have read for personal reasons and which I would like to share with you.

I hope that in some small way at least, this book will respond usefully to valid and current questions in your own life.

ONE

INTRODUCTION:
To Ourselves -
To Loneliness

WE already have lived part of our lives; there is no turning back; the past is irreversible. But it is not lost to us either. Some part of its presence always touches us. I remember a long time ago, when a friend said:

> Sometimes, not often, I live with hope. Or I want to die and then I want to live. Or I can't reach out. Sometimes I feel almost close to the meaning of life, only I can't find what that is.

She was depressed, lonely and very much afraid—but I loved the beauty of her searching mind and I tried to help her find some meaning in her life. Her quest touched me. At times when I was most honest with myself, I admitted that my loneliness had affected me very deeply, too.

Since that time, I have worked with hundreds of other people who are also searching, but who tend to look back and not ahead—who see themselves as having little value, or who have only a vague sense of how to take stock of their own unrecognized potential. It often seems to me that many people feel buried under the pressures of suburban/ urban environments. They live suspended, somewhere between the future, which they cannot reach, and the past that is history only. They are not centered in their present; issues of time and change confuse them. They may be seeking the elusive sense of their own inner heroes, they

1

have not found them. The uncertainties of life leave them unfulfilled and searching. Their disconnectedness disturbs me. Listen. Are these words familiar?

"I am afraid to be alone."
"Nobody cares."
"I don't know how to plan my life."
"Nothing I do has meaning."
"If only I could become involved."

Over the years these voices have haunted me because of the sense of loneliness implied. I kept exploring new ways to help.

Finally, I knew that I already had embarked on a voyage of discovery, an odyssey, to be exact: ". . . a long series of wanderings, especially when filled with notable experiences and hardships." This book is about what happened to me and perhaps what happens to you.

All expeditions start with a dream, evolve into a plan, and move towards a goal. At some subliminal level, I guess one always has a suitcase packed.

I brought to this study some of the tools of my trade—some personal self-doubts: the years of training and practice as a clinician; my earlier years as a professional navigator, ocean voyager, designer/builder, abandoned child. I brought, as well, some deeply affecting knowledge of myself as father, lover, poet, failure, creator, destroyer, joiner, success. "Surely," I thought, "these are enough to begin with."

I had a lot to learn. I did not know how disturbing some of this adventure would be. But I began, knowing somehow that as I shared my experiences with others who had been there, as I pushed deeper into this phenomenon called "loneliness," I would find out more also about who I was. It was almost as though I half expected some day to turn a corner and finally meet myself. I began to spend hundreds of illuminating hours talking and sharing with other people—colleagues, clients, friends, family—people who knew of my project and volunteered to be interviewed on tape, with strangers from as many divergent walks of life as I could manage. And I drew on my life and years of professional experience working with people. I searched out hundreds of related writings by novelists and philosophers, social scientists, educators, psychologists, and others. I went to my friends in education and to people who were totally invested in studying ways of effecting change.

But I wanted to generate answers, not just ask questions. I wanted the experience of loneliness to be illustrated in the direct and honest statements of people who dared to look deeply into their own lives and who would share their feelings with me.

The fact that they did has changed my life.

Loneliness Is a Universal Experience

I have come to believe that we live in a society that unwittingly fosters loneliness. Almost everywhere in our country, loneliness has a negative connotation. The equation often goes like this: to be lonely is to have failed somehow. And feeling lonely often conflicts with such traditional themes of American life as "personal autonomy," "self-sufficiency," and ideas of "self-improvement." If we are lonely we have not succeeded. It's like looking into a mirror and sensing that what you see isn't what you want to see. Conflicts set in. It is because of this that people often take their feelings of loneliness underground. When we can find no one with whom to share, or when we feel we are not meeting our own criteria of competency and success, our feelings are candidates for repression.

Loneliness may well be the most universal and significant experience that we have in common, for loneliness touches us all in some way, some time, some where. We may give different names to it. There appears to be a growing awareness that this experience we call loneliness may be one of the major causes of premature death and emotional difficulty in our country. Certainly the medical and psychological consequences of loneliness can be devastating. For many, loneliness minimally hurts; for others, it may become a crippling and chronically disabling force. It may lead to physical illness, depression, insanity, suicide, paralyzing fear, and withdrawal from any meaningful relationship.

I believe that viewing loneliness from the medically popoular concept of "illness," or as a deficit condition, perpetuates the problem of successfully dealing with it as a phenomenon which is a natural part of everyone's life. There is still a great lack of knowledge and a lot of disagreement about how to deal with loneliness. It is even difficult to come up with an acceptable definition of the word itself. And often those people who are most entrusted with the task of being in the so called "helping professions" in our society are unable to respond.

For millions of people, loneliness remains insidiously present, painfully experienced, frighteningly misunderstood.

So we search for answers to our painful questions surrounded by riddles. We wonder about the universal predicament of our aloneness; and the existential meaning of our life. We are, after all, in many ways imprisoned in our own separate bodies, forever distinctly original and therefore different from any other living person. We deal with issues of our place in the universe, our spirituality, and our own death—and whether anyone will care whether we are gone, or cares that we are here.

We deal with our skin-hunger needs to be close—to touch the warmth of other people, to bury our bodies into or against theirs. Our need is to share and have meaning for and membership with them, to know that somehow we are irreplaceable, even though we are not, as we may have naively believed, the hub of the known universe.

We do not want our hues, our truth scattered like blown leaves across time. We do not want to be lost. When we deal with loneliness we deal with the very essence of our own personhood. We deal in subjective value judgments, in cultural expectations, in dreams and fantasy as well as substance.

At the same time, we do make impressions from the pressure of our bodies; our weight carries as much impact when we are happy as when we are sad. Both our courage and our cowardice lead us toward solutions. We are, reportedly, the only animals with a conscience. So, we are the best of a breed in a nature which can be bountiful and orderly—and our conscience will tell us many things if only we will learn to listen.

TWO

THE LANGUAGE OF LONELINESS

- of myth and metaphor

"The limits of my language *mean the limits of my world.*"

Wittgenstein

SOME time ago, I heard a voice at the end of the line saying, "Hi, how are you doing?" "O.K.," I said, and then impulsively added, "How are you?" I knew the minute I said it that something was wrong.

"I'm fine," came the automatic reply. There was a pause then, and just as I had guessed, a changed, more subdued voice, which was no longer masking, came back to me. "Dick, I feel like I really need to come in and talk with you. I'm really hurting."

Later that evening, after we had talked in my office, I locked up and walked through the rain to where I had parked my car. It had been a long day and I felt tired. I was thinking of the people whom I had talked to, talk which had often centered around their feelings of depression or loneliness.

I wondered where they all were now. I thought to myself, "Do they ever wonder what happens to me between 8:00 p.m. and 9:00 a.m.? What happens to Dick Price when he's not here." I remember, as I write, that I had begun to feel very much alone that night, my mind drifting back to the

7

time of my own hurting, in those boyhood years when I had searched for my natural mother in the back alleys and crazy-quilt steets of Scranton, Pennsylvania—where the "red-light" district used to be. Back then, I had wondered what would happen to me if I could never find her. At the time I did not understand how much *wondering* becomes central to the experience we name "*loneliness*." I know now that I did then what we all often do when the answers to our questions are not forthcoming. I built my own myths about how things would be between my mother and me as a way of making comprehensible something I could not understand and over which I felt no control. I believe we do this a lot when we are lonely. The mythology I created as a young boy was that this unknown mother was very poor and living in shabby conditions somewhere. She had not abandoned me but had been forced to give me up; I the hero, would find her and rescue her.

Like the fairy tale I had created about my mother, our myths are rich in metaphor and build upon unprobable guesses about how things really are or could be. They serve to alleviate our anxiety about these unknowables, and are attempts to reassure ourselves that things really are the way we perceive them. In myth we turn our emotions into visual images that we are familiar with in nature, and in myth we find a way of testing and evaluating our personal history. Yet there are moments in all our lives when such creations conflict with our daily realities. When this occurs our ideal self images undergo often painful re-evaluation and more profound loneliness.

One of the most striking characteristics I have found about feeling lonely is the high degree to which *loneliness involves us in questions of self-worth*. Almost all the people who have told me in any detail about their experiences of loneliness have mentioned self-doubts in connection with being lonely. Even using the word "loneliness" troubled some of them. Whatever else the word implied, it represented also a feeling that they had not wanted, did not like, and which contained a negative connotation for them:

That it was the result of some basic fault, which lay within them, like weaknesses of personality which they felt but had not admitted to anyone else. We try so hard in our lives to be accepted and liked by everyone—we're always evaluating how we are seen.

If you could actually visualize loneliness as a thing and you tried to capture its form with deft brush strokes on canvas, it might come out looking like a huge hole, or perhaps a question mark. I visualize a question mark because loneliness is so full of questions of "Why?" and "How?" and "If only . . ." and when you look at the question-mark symbol, you can see that it is an open-ended, unsymmetrical, curving line with this little dot at the bottom (which may represent us), or a puff of smoke, or a circle which doesn't know how to complete itself? . . .

Someone once said that if we are to understand something, we need to be able to describe it. To do that we need words and the conceptual images that words convey in our mind. More than that, we need the structure of language in order to mull over and process in our mind's eye the impressions and feelings with which we are continually bombarded. *Loneliness, then, is something that we must use words to define, and I believe it is through words that we shape the meaning of loneliness.*

What are some of these descriptive words that we feel and identify with loneliness? Empty? Left out? Restless? Barren? Notice how negative these words are. Such words tend to increase feelings of disconnectedness between ourselves and other less personal things in our environment. When we string word images together into sentences, they often give greater clarity and shape to our feelings as we define them for ourselves and the people we trust to share them with.

It is out of this fusion of language and the images mirroring our feelings that we structure views of our world and our behaviors. If we interpret ourselves as small and helpless, we will be less inclined to challenge or to move boldly toward things that we want. Our feelings become guideposts for us in that they act as a measure of how we are doing and what is happening to us. It doesn't much matter whether we are talking about feelings that relate to visual, tactile, kinesthetic, nonvisual, or other experiences that impact upon our system, since it is through the visual imagery of language that we explain it to ourselves. So, on the one hand, feelings clue us into how things are going, physically and psychologically; on the other hand, they can act to increase our capacity to handle stress when we need to. Our feelings of loneliness, then, can be useful indicators that something in our emotional environment is not as it should be; that we need to make changes— changes that may require our making choices.

I have come to understand that *loneliness* is simply a word that we give to an experience that each of us faces alone, and yet, when we look deeper, we can find common threads that run through all of these individual experiences. We tell ourselves what these experiences mean in words and the way we define these words will indicate where we are in our own lives at that particular time.

We know that we can only define truth for ourselves, that truth is in the eye of the beholder, but we still hope that other people will understand our words when we try to explain our experiences to them. Sometimes we even hope they can explain our experiences and words back to us. This private language system evolves from our basic drive to communicate more than just our minimal wants.

Examining the influence that language has in shaping our feelings (and the meaning that we give to our experiences) seems to me an essential first step in understanding the nature of loneliness. Yet, until now, I believe, this has largely been ignored in examining the experience of loneliness; and it is strange because words are the link between feelings and thought.

Just think about the impact that a word like *schizophrenic* or *alcoholic* or *criminal* would have upon you if suddenly, someone were using it to identify a person you loved. Most often our words come to us first from other people who impart their implied meaning to the words. The words, then, like "loneliness words," already have quality and image, upon which our own feelings and conceptualizations are now overlaid.

Visualizing Our Loneliness Can Help Communicate It to Others

As I write this, I am thinking of a man who told me that he saw himself "dancing a lonely dance in which I was outside of this tight circle of other dancers, who kept opening the circle to let me in, only I kept imagining this thin, hidden membrane that connected each of them, and would hold me out. The other dancers, a lot of them were women, were like a wheel which rolled on and on without me. I kept dancing though, dancing closer and closer to them."

This was how he saw loneliness in his mind's eye. This is how he explained it to himself as well as to me. It was the word-image script his mind wrote, a mythology he structured in his head to try to explain and deal with his feelings of unsureness, feelings both of fear and of hope. What was true for the dancer is true for all of us. We often feel the most threatened about the things we do not know. This is the core of loneliness.

In ancient times the dancer of myths did not know what would happen if he tried to enter the mystical circle his story had created. His myth centered, as they always do, upon himself, and was played out through the word-derived images in his mind—polarities of feelings: fear of rejection by the group, sense of helplessness, and hope for eventual acceptance and personal strength.

Myths, whether ancient or modern, fill the gaps in the unknown; in loneliness, the power of the unknown becomes maximized and ripe for excesses. It is quite possible when we imagine the unknown, to anticipate the worst. Sometimes, for example, when you ask children questions that they know they cannot answer, their responses will be other questions, or answers which have nothing to do with the questions asked.

In some ways we are very like children. It is the inability to find answers that terrifies us and we choose to fill in our ignorance with myth, so our distress may seem less threatening. Myths will always be a part of our lives, because they tap into that creative part of our nature that fosters dreams, visualizations of our forgotten history and of our unknown future.

Yet myths are not wholly lies nor are they complete evasions. Myths, daydreams and plans can become stepping stones in the creative process of viewing possibilities and deciding where we want to go. As long as we also recognize they can be roadblocks to facing reality head-on.

Shortly after I began writing this book, I was interviewing a woman who got so excited about what we were discussing she suddenly jumped up from her chair, saying, "You've got to promise me you'll tell them that loneliness is all it is cracked up to be, and more!" I promised her I would try. We sat together talking for some time after that and toward the end of our meeting, I read her this beautifully metaphoric description of an experience in loneliness written by Thomas Wolfe.

> And left alone to sleep within a shuttered room, with thick sunlight printed in bars upon the floor, unfathomable, loneliness crept through him; he saw his life down the solemn vista of a forest isle, and he knew he would always be the sad one; caged in that little round skull, imprisoned in that beating and most secret heart, his life must always walk down lonely passages. Lost. He understood that men were forever strangers to one another, that no one ever comes really to know anyone, that imprisoned in the dark womb of our mother, we come to life without having seen her face, that we are given to her arms a stranger, and that, caught in that insoluable prison of being, we escape it never, no matter what arms may clasp us, what mouth may kiss us, what heart may warm us. Never, never, never, never . . .

As I finished my reading, I saw that she had begun

crying softly to herself and I waited before speaking again. After a long space of time, she said simply, "I saw myself in that shuttered room, closed away because I had been afraid to reach out. Now I see I have to make a choice."

We had known each other only through her participation in my research project; and yet we both impulsively chose to stand in the middle of that room, holding each other quietly as a way of communicating our shared feeling of the moment. Even after we parked, her words kept repeating in my head because I too believe *choice* is an intrinsic part of how we deal with loneliness and with life.

I often think about this woman who had to make a choice and recognize our common humanity. We do make choices whether we want to or not, since not doing anything is still choosing. One of the concepts we will be examining in this book is that: *Loneliness itself might well be the result of making a choice from any number of alternatives, a choice of certain images in which we might view ourselves as, for example, isolated, unworthy, or somehow unwanted. We might instead have selected from quite another group of alternatives that could have led us toward being with others, feeling satisfied with our relationships and ourselves.*

THREE

SELF-FULFILLING PROPHESIES and BEING "LONELY"

> "What do you do about where you
> are now? Simple. You don't compare
> yourself, you don't criticize yourself,
> you don't condemn yourself. You
> simply go out and find the people
> you have this mutuality with . . ."
>
> Jess Lair

REAL loneliness begins when we feel disconnected, when we realize that no other person can ever *belong* to us, no one can take our place in death, or think and say our thoughts for us now. For a number of people I have known, the most frightening aspect of loneliness is the thought that they might die without another person ever really knowing them, for others it is that they will leave nothing of significance behind. Many of the people I have talked with tell me how boring it is for them to be with themselves for long periods of time and to tap into themselves for any comfort or nourishment.

Many of these people speak of feelings of regret that they will die without ever knowing or "finding" themselves. George Sheehan, the author of *Running and Being*, points out very eloquently an issue that touches us all when he writes, "Thoreau went into the woods because he feared that when he came to die, he would discover that he had

15

never lived." You can see the part that fear plays in these regrets, for *fear and loneliness often go hand in hand.*

People must use words to convey their emotions and thoughts to us. An example I will always remember is of the dark side in the sadness illustrated in my friend Jim's statement about himself:

> To me loneliness has always meant that I've never really been number one or two, or three, in anybody's life. I'm not one of the few people you really miss when they're not there. Now I know people I see more or less regularly, perhaps a dozen, but if I vanish today, it would leave no great gap in any of their lives, and I don't think that there are any of them who will spend a whole lot of time weeping over me. There won't be a hole to fill. Well, unfortunately, the same is also true of me. I mean, I don't think there is any one person or any several people who are that much of my life either, and I sort of feel that's the true definition of loneliness. When other people don't love you, that doesn't make you alone. It's when you don't love them, that you're alone.

Among the Hardest Words to Speak Are Those Related to Loneliness

Words that we use to describe feelings of loneliness are often the hardest words to find or to speak because they are so personal, and we have even more trouble when we imagine that people will view them negatively. A dear friend of mine, Jim, is one of the few people I know who has spent a great deal of time looking specifically at how his own loneliness has developed over the years and then systematically has attempted to find ways to deal with it. I find this trait to be unusual.

I have another friend, Laureen, whose responses to her own pain are more common. She had never told anyone about how desperately lonely she was until the first time she agreed to an interview with me. Laureen had hidden this bit of herself from her few acquaintances. At work she sometimes ate lunch with a few of the other secretaries from her office and they would talk about their weekends, or what their vacations had been like, or about how this or that date or marriage was going, and other somewhat personal events, but mostly, Laureen lied about what she did. She created a myth about her life outside of the office that didn't match the fact that she spent most of her time going alone to movies, reading or watching T.V. in her apartment. She saw this as a necessary part of her disguise, since she didn't like the way she felt about herself and thought that othr people would not like her if they knew who she really was. She occasionally slept with men for whom she had only mild affection, in the hope that somehow this would fill her need for closeness and intimacy. Each time had left her ashamed of her physical needs and more entrenched in her feelings of failure than before. Now, at age twenty-eight, she had finally begun to face the pain of her loneliness.

I can remember her words very clearly. "It really helps to say it. I'm lonely. I don't know what to do about it, yet, but it really helps to get it out and put it into words. For so long, I wouldn't even say it. . . ."

I have often found that people don't trust their words, because they are afraid that if they say what is on their minds others won't understand, or worse, what they say might be viewed as not good enough. Like the time I asked Beth Thomas, a fifty-eight year-old woman I had known for years, if she would be willing to do a taped interview about loneliness.

I had asked her what the word *loneliness* meant to her. Beth started to answer, then hesitated for a long moment, perplexed. Finally, she said, "Why don't you just give me written questions and I'll answer each one for you, in writing." When I told her it would be better for me to do the interviews live, and on tape, she seemed to struggle with some indecision. Finally she said, "I haven't been lonely in a long time. I'm not sure what loneliness is. Maybe first I'll look up the word in the dictionary. Somebody must know what it is; people use the word all the time."

I think there's a lot of Beth in all of us. We wonder what people will say if we expose ourselves. Will we measure up? Or, we think there must be somebody around who knows more than we do. We do all this wondering in our minds trying to fit language to our thoughts. In a way, the quality of our life is expressed by the meaning we give to these difficult to speak words. Our happiness and our sadness is bound up in the images they illustrate for us.

Words can be a lubricant. Such a simple invitation as, "How about dropping in for a cup of coffee?" may draw a word picture of a pleasant time sharing, or it may contain a deeper meaning which is only indirectly implied: "I am lonely and I need someone to be with me." We each view this picture differently depending on our own inner feelings and often the picture in our minds is not the one perceived by the person to whom we reveal it.

Yet is through our language that we can construct images of hope and trust for ourselves as well as for those in our world. Our minds select words and turn them into images from which we compare and reshuffle the ideas that gradually shape our personal identities. Without language how can we communicate what we stand for, or stand for what we communicate?

Roadblocks to Understanding Loneliness

But, I believe that bias has crept into the meaning attached to loneliness and the words we use to speak about it. This is not so strange, since many of these words were developed by people trained in the medical sciences, as these were the first disciplines to attempt to begin systematically investigating loneliness; for example, doctor, patient, disease (of loneliness), sickness, pathology, cure, etc. These are words from a scientific orientation for people trained to deal with illness, not health.

Such disciplines treat "people problems" that already have happened, by attempting to categorize disease so that

the "malignancy" can be medicated, cut out, or repaired surgically. With this kind of thinking and nomenclature it certainly could be frightening for anyone unlucky enough to admit to the "disease" of loneliness.

I emphasize this to illustrate how strongly the meanings given to such words influence one's feelings about being lonely. There is a bias in these words, especially since they derive their meaning from the expectation that in order to get "well," we must already be "sick."

After working with hundreds of people, I have concluded that feeling lonely doesn't mean you're sick. You may *feel* sick because of some misperceptions we all have about equating emotional problems with "illness," and with labels like "neurosis." When something is wrong you go to a doctor who "treats" with the intention of "curing." Unwittingly, a lot of people think problems involving the mind, "mental problems" (which are really only problems of living), should be solved in the same way. It's too bad, because so many people are conditioned to feel: "I must be sick to feel lonely. I need to get some professional help in order to be well again."

Often I believe people solve their own loneliness problems. (This isn't to deny that people may have made the correction assessment of their incapacity to attempt it without professional help. The professionals often have been useful and they may be needed.) The tragedy is that the medically-oriented approach may also lead the "ill" person to feel a helpless victim. After all, we can't be blamed for catching cancer, or "mono," or even the common cold sometimes. On this basis, one can reason that we are not so responsible for cowardice, shirking of responsibilities, evasive manner, putting ourselves down, or making life miserable for our spouses or children. As a *victim*, we do not have to make changes, our past is to blame: fathers who did not love us well enough, parents who separated and left us alone, friends who lied to us. "It wasn't our fault, it was theirs . . . If only things had been better. . . ."

Our friends and relatives surely understand when we need a liver operation, or our appendix removed for health reasons, but we feel other people will perceive our emotional pain as caused because we didn't try hard enough, were strange ducks and weren't managing well, or we just don't have "it" (whatever "it" is). And that's a "three-strikes is out" count. Whether the impact of these analogies affects us profoundly or only slightly, I believe the fact remains that they imply a serious, yet unprovable, implication of failure that can and does affect many people's lives.

At some point in our lives, many people feel if they could only hand over the function of problem areas in their lives to those professional groups who were better equipped to understand such matters, these problems could be solved. This is the era of specialization, after all. But there is a problem here that has to do with our desire to abdicate responsibility to find some magical elixir or person when such a potion or person probably doesn't exist.

In any case, when we have abdicated our own reasoning power and, instead, embraced the experts' definition because we do not trust ourselves, it is very difficult to reclaim our right to define our own reality. Thus, once it becomes a habit not to seek solutions for our own distress but rather to choose either the advice of others and then feel unsatisfied though they offered us nothing but the best they had. One way I believe we can rid ourselves of distrust is by allowing ourselves to embrace self-responsibility and to look at the larger, less-medical and more-encompassing perspective of loneliness as part of the human condition.

There are other influences that add to the dis-ease of feeling lonely in our country. They come from our pioneering, adventurous backgrounds and the myths we build around them, as well as the importance we have placed upon such things as competitive drive and being successful. When I think of the word "competition" now as I write, I see a technicolor moving picture, composed of thoughts, and feeling images, words and sounds, etc., flashing through my head. I can see people being "competitive":

men and women at work, pushing for results; numbers flashing on the big boards of stock exchanges; runners straining to pass others in the drive to become "number one." In five seconds, for example literally hundreds of word images streak by. Many of these are metaphors, such as that of the runners, which inherently carry in their subjective meanings for me predictions about the future.

Also, identification with such words as weak and strong, "failure" and "success" has great cultural impact on what it means to be lonely in our country. People often feel there is a great shame in being lonely. Almost without exception, all the individuals I interviewed about these feelings found it hard to share their lonely feelings with friends and acquaintances. None of us wants to be judged "weak" or "different" in the negative sense. It often seems safest to appear like everybody else. We try so hard to discover and maintain acceptable behavior. Yet one of the developmental tasks we all face in growing up is to find a real identity for ourselves that makes us unique and authentic, to build upon the rich magical inner world of our own myths, fantasies and dreams and, at the same time, to be part of our fellow human beings.

I think one poignant episode described in the story of John Thomas Merrick, titled *The Elephant Man and Other Remembrances* by Sir Frederic Treves, emphasizes what being seen as "different" can mean to a human being craving acceptance. John Merrick was born with a grotesquely large, misshapen head, and other physical deformities that were repulsive to most people. As an adult he was viewed as a "freak" and put on public exhibition for money. Because of the size of his head, Merrick could not manage to sleep in a "normal" lying position, but instead, had to sleep sitting up. His one special friend was Dr. Frederick Treves, a surgeon, who helped Merrick deal with these deformities during the last three years of his life.

In telling of Merrick's death, Dr. Treves explains that Merrick had often told him how much he wished that it would be possible for him to lie down in bed to sleep "like other people" did. On his last, fatal night he must have tried vainly to do just that. However, when he put his huge head on the soft pillow it must have fallen backward because of its weight and dislocated his neck. Thus, the forlorn wish to be "like other people" that had dominated his life, was the tragic cause of death.

Often, in this country, the person who spends his or her life alone is viewed as having been left at the starting gate in the great American game of "pairing-up."

"See that poor woman sitting alone over there at that table? Probably no one to go home to. Wonder what she must be thinking? Kind of sad, huh?" Our first image of the person alone is of someone who has not managed well. Being longely is not O.K., any more than being "weak" is as O.K. as being "strong." Still, historically Americans are supposed to be independent; we *should* be able to "stand on our own two feet" and develop that personal self-sufficiency, that individual autonomy that gives us "freedom of self-expression" and "individual mastery." These two images battle each other, often to the point of absurdity and they will continue to do so as long as we believe other people's view of us and doubt our own.

We Cannot Do What We are Unable to Visualize

Combating self-distrust requires learning how to create our own ideal images, to see ourselves differently. We can't make changes in our loneliness, or anything else, until we first visualize what those changes we want so badly might be. The thought is father to the deed.

When I began to consider writing this book, I pictured a number of lonely people whom I felt close to and then saw them finding something in my words that would be meaningful for them. Afterwards, I let my thoughts go and trusted the positive energy of my imagination.

Can you allow yourself to accept the notion that our minds and our thoughts are really pure energy—energy which we direct. When we permit our minds to trust in our ability to control our lives, we start a flow of energy that can overcome any doubting, "I'll believe it when I see it," attitudes that we may have started with.

If you have any doubts about the existence of this energy of the mind, you might try a simple experiment. Tie a small but solid weight to the end of a two-foot piece of string. Sitting comfortably in your chair, with your elbow resting on the arm of the chair to keep it still, hold the weighted string so that it hangs in front of you. Keeping your hand steady, begin to visualize the weight starting to move without your physically moving it. Concentrate hard. Visualize the weight beginning to swing with increasing energy toward and away from you in a straight arc as you repeat over and over in your mind the thought, "Out and back, out and back, out and back, like the steady swing of a pendulum." Later you might also visualize the pendulum shifting from left to right, or around and around in circles.

Let's unravel your string of belief a bit further. The pendulum experiment was a simplistic way of demonstrating the mind's ability to effect change. It is analogous to our letting go of engrained habits. Loneliness will remain until we are able to visualize giving it up for something else. We'll see this "something else" when we believe in it enough. Somehow there must be this leap of self-faith or we cannot succeed in overcoming our own pain.

Finally, it becomes a question of choice. That's what the following chapters in this book are about. They're about giving up one thing to gain another. They're about you and me, and lots of others, choosing or not choosing to believe in and use our own God-given energy in a new way to make valuable changes in our lives.

FOUR

THE LONELINESS PRINCIPLE

> If there is any answer to the meaning
> of life, it does not lie out there some-
> place, but within me. Life does not
> present me with meaning. Life
> merely is. . . .
>
> Author Unknown

"YOU see it all the time," people say, shrugging slightly, as though it were a fact that had nothing to do with them. Loneliness just isn't something people talk about very much, admit to, or write about. Yet loneliness is indigenous to our way of life, and to an enormous, if uncharted extent, growing numbers of people live painfully with it.

When I interviewed Robert Weiss, sociologist and author, and member of the faculty of Harvard University, he pointed out a good example of this prevailing condition. He related that of all those thousands of books on the shelves of the library at Harvard, his book, *Loneliness— The Experience of Emotional and Social Isolation*, was one of the most frequently stolen. I believe that this tells us something of immeasurable value. People are hungry for information about loneliness.

Why? Part of the answer is eloquently described by Suzanne Gordon in her book, *Lonely In America:*

> Life in America has exploded, and loneliness is one main ingredient of the fallout. What was once a philosophical problem, spoken mainly by poets and prophets, has now become an

25

almost permanent condition for millions of Americans, not
only for the old or divorced, but also for the men and women
filling singles bars and encounter groups, the adolescents running away from home or refusing to go to school, the corporate
transients who move every two or three years, and the people
calling suicide and crisis hotlines in search of someone to talk
to. Knowing no limits of class, race or age, loneliness is today
the great leveler, a new American tradition. . . .

*William Glasser, psychiatrist, and author of The Iden-
tity Society,* estimates that over 50 percent of people who
visit physicians go with non-medical complaints which
have more to do with painful problems of living, and
unresolved issues of personal relationship. Frankly, I am
surprised that reports like this are only now beginning to
be substantiated. Hospital "hotlines," or example, are
finally beginning to discover and report publicly that loneliness appears to have leap-frogged over alcoholism, drug
abuse and other concerns to become a leading problem of
the day. Many authorities believe also that coronary artery
disease may no longer head the list of people-problems
often referred to as "self-inflicted, life-style diseases."

When you add the people who do not solve these problems for themselves, but instead seek help from their law-
yer, minister or rabbi, or at their private or public mental
health clinic and counseling center, the plethora of emotional pain and suffering taking place in our country becomes quite evident.

This is only the top of the emotional vortex as I see it, for
below the surface, hidden and feeling alone are the un-
counted millions more who hide their misery in unfulfilling social relationships, marriages of little comfort, boring
jobs, etc. During their lifetimes, they continue to feel
trapped and lonely. Yet true to the American tradition of
independence they hide the loneliness and live as Thoreau
said "lives of quiet desperation."

When you get close to people who are hurting, and when
they trust you, you find that most of the hurt is a hunger for

a meaningful relationship. What is missing from most lonely lives is a close and satisfying human contact with some other person. Loneliness can come when something is missing or seems so, even if what appears lost is only one's self-confidence in personal relationships, or something which one had hoped for but which didn't materialize.

Look at the personal want ads in the back of many newspapers and many magazines. You will find that almost everything advertised there is an attempt to alleviate loneliness; from computer-date matching and escort services to the swinging singles and sex clubs, dating bars, massage parlors, and the "beautiful women eager to meet you." Perhaps the saddest of these personal pleas for companionship are legitimate and yet sad personal-column ads for soul-mates, paid for by lonely persons trying to convey how personable they are to that special someone out there that they have never met, but who they hope will be induced to respond. Think about those ads for a moment—and about yourself, or people that you know who might compose such ads at some desprate time. Read the classified ads in the *Singles Sections* of weekly papers sold from coin boxes along the streets in affluent and sun-blessed Santa Monica, California:

WYOMING

Shy, Wyoming Rancher, bachelor, 43 looking for a White attractive, sincere woman, 29-35. Must be affectionate, not bossy and finds ranchlife compatible. Divorcee with children O.K., but must be a one-man-wife and all former marital ties severed. This virile Taurus is 6'11" 170 lbs., brown eyes and brown hair with grey. I am considered nice-looking, kind and affectionate. I have worked hard to build my sheep ranch and now find coming home to empty ranch house intolerable. When corresponding, send photo, please.

BAY AREA

I NEED a lady, 20 to 30 who is as lonely as I. I'm 27, live in San Francisco area, am an EET, love swimming, poetry, movies, music, fireplaces and beaches. Each letter from a sincere lady answered. Photo appreciated.

Illustrated here is the real-life need to find someone to feel connected to, something beyond ourselves, and spelled out in these personal ad sections is the undeniable power of hope. Similarly, just listen to the popular music on the radio, saturated as it is with moods of yearning, of lost love, of need.

Not only what we listen to but other elements of our personal environments echo this need. Why are we so concerned about how we dress? Of course, we want people to know that we keep ourselves clean and tidy, we want to present ourselves well to others, but why? Why all this need to appear so attractive, or successful, or sporty, or sexy, or so completely together? There are numerous secondary reasons of course, but the overriding one is always the same—it comes from the innate and fundamental drive not to be the lonely one among a world of interconnected people.

For example, X-rated theaters thrive in every city in this country. Why? I believe that as explicit and mechanical as these films are, what they sell is much more than sex; they capitalize on loneliness, and it's big business, with thousands of hawkers peddling "cures." For a brief period of time they offer at least the illusion of intimacy and caring to thousands of people who are unsatisfied with their own interpersonal or non-existent relationships. It seems to me the only reason more women aren't going into these places is because it is still more taboo for them than for men. But it is a prophetic commentary on our society that, while the mercenary, pornographic dealers advertise S-E-X, they are really among the first to respond actively to the compelling and enormous phenomenon of loneliness. Whether we live on farms, in the suburbs, or in the city, it is still somehow easier for us to talk about sex than to talk about being lonely. We hear allusions and jokes made about sex every day, and we can see the humorous side of sex and accept its caprices as well as its importance. Things are quite different when we come to talking about being lonely, because we've learned to be ashamed and frightened of delving deeply into our own painful feelings.

For better or worse, the calculating merchants of sex have read people very well, I think, for they have recognized that at some deep level all of this is not funny at all, and can at times be very sad. They appreciate, too, that there is comfort, small and cold as it may be, in recognizing that you are not alone in being lonely.

What Does This Mean When You Yourself Are Lonely?

Contrary to the slick and well-satisfied exteriors that millions of Americans feel they must present, there lies an internal confusion and distress among many people that is much more common than realized. It is an unnatural and damaging condition. This process of denial, and the resulting core of anxiety that accrues comes largely out of misunderstanding the nature of loneliness as a life force; it is increased by the feelings of failure which have been attached to being lonely.

Time and again as people share their inner feelings with me, I find them reflecting with some sadness over their sense of isolation from someone they care about. Often they express it this way: "No matter how close I manage to feel with someone, it never seems enough, or it doesn't last the way I want it to." There is generally a constant, sometimes muted underlying theme to what they are saying; it is the contrasting fear of being left alone on the one hand, and, on the other, the gnawing, unacceptable realization that no matter how intensely close we may come to another person for a time, we are each separate identities, we must also face the impossible eradication of our aloneness and our eternal potential for loneliness. This final loneness, then, is not just culturally or environmentally determined, and our conscious perception of loneliness is not simply the result of some failure on our part. Neither can we merely lay the blame for our alienation from each other on current changes in lifestyles the fact that we live in a precarious world of eroding family structures, which seem less stable than before. And yet, this is what we have often tended to do. It has needlessly harmed us, because there has been a deepening fear that things are getting worse instead of better, that our aloneness and loneliness is an out-of-control, mushrooming phenomenon of modern times. We reinforce this lonely, helpless position each time we say, "I'm only one person, I can't change things. I can't change society?" Or when, in our devotion to individuality, we set ourselves apart, and then wonder why we feel so isolated? But every day that I talk in depth with people I find an even more authentic truth emerging. It may be partially obscured under layers of conscious or unconscious awareness, but when we trust ourselves we can also recognize that far from being largely an 18th, 19th, or 20th century phenomenon, loneliness has somehow always been at the core of our lives, that loneliness has been the central underlying theme of Man/Woman since we first were able to communicate, and perhaps before. It is a condition of human be-ing.

In his poem, *The Creation,* James Wheldon Johnson writes about the old-time Negro preachers who spoke or sang of the need for companionship in their inspirational sermons. Rhythmically intoning the words, perhaps with music and the stomping and hand-clapping of the congregation to accompany him, the old-time preacher swings into the sermon:

> And God stepped out on space,
> And He looked around and said:
> I'm lonely -
> I'll make me a world. . .

> Then God walked around,
> and God looked around
> On all that He had made
> And He looked at His sun,
> And He looked at His moon,
> And He looked at His little stars;

He looked on His world
With all its living things,
And God said: "I'm lonely still."

Then God sat down -
On the side of the hill where He could think;
By a deep, wide river He sat down;
With His head in His hands,
God thought and thought,
Till He thought: "I'll make me a man!"

Up from the bed of the river
God scooped the clay
And by the bank of the river
He kneeled Him down;
And the Great God Almighty,
Who lit the Sun and fixed it in the sky,
Who flung the stars to the most far corners of the
    night,
Who rounded the earth in the middle of His hand;
This Great God;
Like a mammy bending over her baby,
Kneeled down in the dust
Toiling over a lump of clay
Till He shaped it in His own image;

Then into it He blew the breath of life,
And Man became a living soul.
Amen. Amen.

We can look back even further than the words of these
old-time preachers when we talk of the need not to be left
alone. We have only to identify with anguished words
spoken from a Cross: "My God, My God, why hast Thou
forsaken me?" I think that even our own fear of death is not
so much in the dying as being dead alone. Even when we
talk of immortality, it seems we never choose to think of
being immortal alone.

The Desire for Permanent Companionship

If there has been one golden dream thoughout the centuries, it is for something permanent—something that we can always be a part of. Consider the more fundamental need behind all artistic or creative efforts, for example. What is the purpose when we write a poem, paint a picture, compose music? To clarify something? To add something new, to express ourselves and to enlarge upon our own sense of mastery? I believe so. Do we make art to add to or to complete ourselves? Yes. For the pleasure of accomplishing something which we can both recognize as ours and yet share with others? Again, I believe so, and yet the living proof is in the experience.

Bob Benvenuto, a former student of mine, has written a powerful testimony to this point in his unpublished manuscript, *Loneliness and Creative Expression*:

> I mentioned that in the beginning of my self-imposed solitude, I ran from myself. I was running from the confusion that was filling in my new isolation. Out of this confusion I picked up some drawing materials and drew a self-portrait . . . It never occurred to me that any type of art would be an outcome of aloneness. Drawing this self-image created a sense of order for me out of the chaos of my new solitude. I felt that I took a progressive step forward by taking hold of these conflicts and given them emotion on paper. I resolved some of my anxiety through art. The drawing is a restoration process that enables me to face my inner images, which were starting to surface because of my aloneness . . .

I would add my own observation to this statement by pointing out that something else happens through the creation of art which is often its most tangible but greatest reward. The artist uses this medium to experience its appreciation by other persons as a confirming sign that he is not alone.

Paulo Knill, a concert musician, artist, therapist, teacher and friend, sums up another aspect of these needs in his thesis, *Expressive Therapies and Education*:

To be connected to myself and my fellow humankind is for me the spiritual issue in my art. If there is a concept of God, it is my brothers, sisters, and me living together in a way that allows for the satisfaction of our primal organismic needs. In this sense it is materialistic dialectic as well as spiritual when I try to perceive most intensely the world by experiencing myself truly as a part of us, the people.

This reminds me of the snow-stranded truck driver I once met in an all-night diner just off Interstate 95 North. He said that being able to talk over his "CB" radio had added ten years to his driving life. With his "CB" he felt connected in a "universal brotherhood" which helped him have an identity of his own, but still belong to something larger than himself.

My wife Jean speaks of her "small visits" with her mother when they call each other every Thursday evening year in and year out. I think it's more than just keeping in touch. For her, it's keeping a boundary of connection with her early life. Such connections are like a lifeline in a sense, a thin wire thread that assures you you're you; just hearing someone talk reinforces that sense of your whole-ness. It's also saying, "You're important to me, we still exist together, we continue to love each other."

Everyone wants to be important to someone else; we each have developed extraordinary ways of trying to obtain this reassurance. Elvira Pratt is no exception, and when she talked with me, she defined herself as that "un-loved spinster on Shawmut Road." She saw herself as being on no one's "People I would like to be with" list, and yet, as she spoke about her lonely life, she also told me of her fearful fantasies of the imaginary seducer who lurked in the night-time shadows of her room. And she said some-thing else that I will never forget: "When the neighbor-hood kids run up on my porch and bang on my door, or they call me names like 'Dragon Lady,' at least I know I'm alive. Little do the children suspect that their taunts tell me I'm special."

The Need to Deny Loneliness

Times change, but our basic needs do not. We can best prove this to ourselves by answering our own questions such as "What do I need most in my life? Why do I need this?"

These days we are certainly more accustomed than ever before to looking inward at our psychological processes. In a way we could say that this is the new American preoccupation, popularized, I suppose by Sigmund Freud, whose genius gave us new ways to view with fascination our own internal functioning. We were enchanted by words like "ego," "id," and "super-ego," as illustrative extensions of those parts of our thinking processes we already sensed but didn't know how to visualize functionally; the id for example, representing that part of us that seeks only ongoing and unbridled pleasure no matter what the consequence. Or, if we consider that in terms of Freudian principles the super-ego (representing that part of our mind that internalizes and evaluates society's ethical and moral beliefs) has the prime function of avoiding pain, it is easy to see why any loss or threat to our happiness. Such as, becoming lonely, would create in us both a physical and emotional defensive response at some level.

Freud looked deeply into the dynamic interplay of both physical and psychological forces and drives that motivate behavior. He was one of the first to see that those clues to personal imbalance that we call symptoms were really the expression not only of the body's unsuccessful attempt to adapt to stress, but the mind's as well, and that these two separate aspects were inextricably (psychosomatically) connected to the person's total (holistic) environment.

In terms of adding our understanding of the dynamics of loneliness I think it is unfortunate that Freud's background was so medically oriented: I believe this led him to misunderstand some human dynamics that are fundamental. This same error continued to be compounded by those who followed him, and in fact, largely continues to this day in such a way as to contribute greatly to what I believe are questionable assumptions, unnecessary mystery, and pain in the experience of loneliness. Most theories of modern psychiatry continue to lump peoples' emotional problems into categories within the spectrum of *pathology*. George Sheehan points up one of the many problems of such labeling when he says: "When I become 'ill' I become a skeptic. What has hitherto been certainty becomes perhaps; what was perhaps becomes maybe; and what was maybe becomes probably not."

What Freud apparently failed to understand (or certainly did not emphasize) was that our sexual (libidinal) drives in particular, and our aggressive drives in general, are not the primary forces which motivate our thoughts and behaviors but in fact are secondary to the more fundamental, all-encompassing drive not to be lonely.

There is a strange paradox to be observed in all this. While Freud was struggling and continually revising his sometimes-ridiculed theories, he apparently experienced extreme feelings of isolation and non-acceptance, both as a practitioner of a new and controversial therapy and as an "outsider," a Jew living in Vienna at a sensitive time in history. Freud spoke publicly of his own loneliness only once, before the B'nai B'rith Association on the day he celebrated his seventieth birthday. At that time it was a plea for acceptance and respite from his own feeling of aloneness.

Perhaps at times, "little knowledge *is* a dangerous thing," because, although Freud and others opened new vistas of the mind to us, many people become so awed by the apparent complexity of his explanations that they are humbled and a bit timid about their own ability to control their destinies. Our dilemma is described very well, I think, by Pamela Staffier in her doctoral dissertation, *The Philosophical Implications of Freud's Psychology*:

> In the eighteenth lecture of his "General Introduction to Psychoanalysis," Freud remarked that humanity has suffered three major insults at the hands of science. The first was when

the earth was shown to be not the center of the universe but
merely a relatively small body revolving round the central sun.
Later, science deepened the universe in every direction,
weighed the stars and measured ever more vast galaxies, and
each advance in knowledge brought home to man with increasing emphasis the physical insignificance of his own home.
. . . The second came when Darwin, with the aid of some
predecessors and contemporaries, dashed man's belief in his
special creation and placed him in the common line of descent
with other animal life. And finally, the third outrage was
modern psychology, in showing man that he is not even master
in his own home, that the self he thought he knew is only a
segment of his real self, that a large and important part of that
real self is almost unknown to him, buried in the unconscious
and guessed at only by inference from scanty hints and brief
flashes of insight.

All of this may at first seem very intimidating indeed.
However, I believe that we now need to sweep away the
mental cobwebs that linger in our minds about that sub-
terranean subconscious life that often seems to lie beyond
our grasp. In some important ways it has been greatly
over-valued and should no longer be used as an excuse for
feeling that we don't know enough already about ourselves
to take charge of things. My own feeling is that often too
much unproductive searching and suffering is spent trying to ascertain deep-seated causes, or blaming our present
situation on our childhood. Many times this fruitless exploration only increases the habit of fear. Besides, it might
be comforting to know that there is little proof to substan-
tiate the belief that people who are trained in exploring the
mind: college professors, physicians, psychologists, et al,
are any less susceptible to loneliness (or even suicide) than
anyone else. In fact, take comfort in the knowledge that in
whatever educational or intellectual category you find
yourself, you have about the same capacity to manage
loneliness as anyone else, possibly better, since some of
the highest incidences of suicide are among people whom
society generally assumes "have it all together." If you are

comparing yourself to others, don't be intimidated. It is not so much the kind of knowledge we have of the origins of our suffering as the way that we grapple with whatever are our problems that is important to our well-being.

I believe we each have an inner sense of what is good for us. And despite our fears we have enough knowledge to begin to deal with loneliness more honestly. Deep down inside, most of us have a moral light. When we are feeling bored or anxious or lonely, part of us knows that some need is not being met. We have some knowledge of the source of our anger and our jealousies and our fears. We can choose to accept that although we are each actually, and existentially alone, we can learn to understand and manage our loneliness. We are, after all, pilgrims traveling the same road; we have not arrived yet, and life offers each of us opportunities for building those delicate and rewarding membranes of caring between us. I feel we can learn to stop feeling that "nobody else is lonely, and seeing ourselves as failures.

Loneliness is more than a conscious awareness; it has an inner meaning, too. When we are looking for something to grasp that makes sense, some simple truth that we can count on, some unchangeable principle that will help us understand why we feel the way we do, and act the way we act, we can look to this existential meaning of loneliness and find one of the categorical principles in life. Philosopher Ben Mijuskovic points this out beautifully in his book *"Loneliness in Philosophy, Psychology and Literature."* He states:

> "I am convinced that enforced loneliness is the dominant theme in Western Civilization. . . . I have argued that loneliness is an elemental structure—an activity or force—within the human psyche . . . ."

He goes on to write of philosophers and others who have grappled with the principle that loneliness has always been the primary awareness of man's consciousness; and is therefore, the major motivating force in life. . . . He says it so well:

> "Loneliness is the prism through which we see the entire spectrum of human life reflected in its multiform attempts to transcend the very feeling of isolation by communications with an other. . . ."

I believe that to understand universal loneliness as the major motivation of all our behaviors is to free us from considerable apprehensions about ourselves. Once we accept this idea we can also recognize that, as Mijuskovic and others have suggested, we need water, food, the ability to breathe air, because these are biological and physiological necessities, but we have one more equally important inner "drive" which is as much a force in our lives as any other.

This is the drive to avoid loneliness. It is more pressing that the drive to obtain sex and love, but it is a part of the need for love and sex, for together they provide us with the pleasures of feeling protected, as well as connected to other persons. I believe the motivating drive not to be lonely is stronger than our aggressive drives. *Our behaviors are conditioned upon our striving to reduce this universally-experienced condition, which is a part of life.*

By accepting the commonality of this experience, its normalcy, we can begin to see ourselves as not "defective" when we meet loneliness along life's path. If we can accept this condition as a reality and take responsibility in relation to how we manage it we can have compassion for ourselves. For me, knowing is always better than not knowing, and reality is always less frightening than the unknown. I've chosen to accept my separate aloneness. In fact, this makes me appreciate all the more how necessary people are to me and how, with very little effort but more attention and sensitivity, I can improve my relationships with people I really want to be close to.

Accepting is a word I like because it implies a calmness after decision. I have decided that loneliness will never trick me again. Accepting that human beings are both metaphysically and existentially alone brings us closer, I think, to that place where we don't have to struggle against solitariness hopelessly. We can stop viewing it as some momentary and terrifying interloper.

I am reminded of what Claire Weekes, in her book, *Agoraphobia*, explains about people's fear, because it applies to loneliness: "The surest way to permanent recovery is to know how to face and cope with panic and not placate it with props."

She goes on to suggest that the first step in dealing with panic is to analyze the process of what is happening to us, and to realize that what we feel when we panic is not so much the object itself we visualize, but the fear of the panic's return. Similarly, in a sense we are dealing with two fears in loneliness. First is the fear of what it *might* be like if we remain lonely, and the second and most inhibiting fear is our anticipation that the fear (or panic) *might* return. It is this second fear, then, which is simply speculation on our part, that keeps our first fear alive and possibly increasing. You might say we are always holding our breaths, worrying about what might happen. And the trick is in acceptance, challenging the fear to do its worst without our backing away. My experience in working with lonely people is that not facing what we fear is ten times worse than facing it. When we call fear's bluff, we usually find that the panic will not increase but will, in fact, subside.

When I think of this aspect of fear connected to loneliness, I always remember my experience with Marguery Tait, a bright, young college student, who came to my office because she was feeling very anxious and lonely. It was our first meeting and no sooner had she come through the door than she began holding her head between her hands as though it might fall off. She immediately began to cry, and swayed as though she would fall. Her first words were, "Oh, I know I'm going to faint!" And, in fact, she obviously planned to do just that. I could feel her preparing to collapse. I remember saying as calmly as I could at the time, "Marguery, please do one thing first. I want you to faint right here, right in the exact center of this rug." Then I added quickly and with bated breath, "Please make yourself faint right this minute, because we don't have much time left for trying to solve your problem, do we?" It worked, because she didn't faint. Suddenly she had to confront her anxiety in a new way and it gave her control over it rather than it controlling her. What she had really meant to express was that her anxiety made her *feel* faint and powerless, not that she *would* faint. After this instance we were able to work through her problem. I taught her to challenge these anxious feelings the next time she felt them by practicing with her some farcial challenges, which she developed until we both broke up with laughter. The one she seemed most delighted with was where she would dramatically stomp her foot on the floor, and looking up as though fear had body and substance, would shout loudly, "O.K., fear, come and get me! I'm opening my big arms to hold you, fear! I'll crush you 'cause I'm stronger than strong, I'm cleaner than clean. I'm ninety-nine and forty-four one-hundredths percent stronger than you are, fear!" Marguery sends me a note or a card now and then. The last one was signed "Lily White," but I knew who it was from.

When we're anxious we are also susceptible to fatigue and irritability and people around us suffer, so it is important for us to understand how this depressive nucleus we call feeling lonely may affect us.

We do not need to *escape* from loneliness. We are not, after all, marionettes controlled by something outside of ourselves, and there is no real difference between what we do and what happens. When we accept the natural place of loneliness in the scheme of things and use it, I believe that we begin with an invaluable organizing principle which will be useful for the remainder of our lives. Accepting the principle of loneliness can change your life. Clearly it puts things in your own hands. You may be thinking, "If it's this simple, why didn't people see it all the time?" And maybe you start wondering if there isn't some huge mistake that you're not seeing. With me it is a question of testing it and each time I do, I step further through the psychological barrier. I think it is a simple question of homework and how much I practice what I believe. The key to my failure or success in dealing with loneliness is *attitude.*

Loneliness is Neither Good Nor Bad

For me, things can only get easier when I really understand something in a way that touches my philosophical self and I see that it will help me. Then I can look at things more objectively too. Perhaps it will be to see that where we are is simply where we are and that to push against nature is to defeat ourselves, since we are a part of nature. If we wish to change ourselves we can learn to do so within the flow of nature and not outside of it. Loneliness is a philosophical concept, too, as well as a part of nature. Within this acceptance of our place in nature we can also understand that loneliness is neither "good" or "bad," that it is both an internal event and an external, in-the-real-world, condition. Certainly, then, it is not purely a psychological phenomenon with which we are dealing.

Feeling Connected to the World Around Us

When we struggle to alleviate loneliness we are dealing with a condition of life which is a force of nature, and we cannot separate these any more than we can our relationship to loneliness. To fight either can only create anxiety and a sense of distance from ourselves. It is important not to get caught up in this sometimes arrogant position that trips up so many people. It is the view that we live on this world like a conqueror upon its shores, rather than our coming out of and being a part of its essence. When I feel my connectedness to nature and to earth, to life growing around me, to my own contribution to its developing presence, then I feel *connected* and a part of something larger than myself. We are lonely when we don't feel comfortably grounded. Things seem complicated, so far away. I think this is why I admire the philosophy and the prophecies of the early American Indians so much. First, because they were able to accept a simple philosophy of life and live within it, satisfied that it was satisfying, that it explained life and the elements.

Secondly, when I think of my own desire not to be lonely, I am comforted and refreshed by the Indian perspective of being grounded in nature. When I am able to experience myself as an extension (or rather a part) of nature, it connects me with my own essence. I too am a part of the Tree of Life, as the Indians describe it, because of this I don't feel so alone. It is vitally important to me to be in touch with what my own philosophy of life is. Do I view myself as a "Searcher?" "Follower?" "Doer?" If next year was cancelled, what would I do today? How do I live my own philosophy? I ponder these questions. They are more useful usually than worrying about psychology.

And I like to listen, too. . . .

Placing oneself in a universal context rather than a personal one may alleviate feelings of loneliness. Try to listen with your inner eyes and to ponder this Zen meditation guide scene. Visualize it in moments of inner distress and anxiety and you may gain self comfort or objective calmness.

"Let your mind be as a crystal clear stream and let your gaze rest on the bottom of that stream.

Let any thoughts you have be as a fish in the stream, which you observe with tender interest and let go."

In a quiet scene such as this thoughts become less muddied and more encouraging. It is like being washed clean again. Be truthful with yourself and thereby gain the new energy that honesty always brings.

I have tried to understand Indian culture and how it relates to me as well as to this study of Loneliness. I listen keenly, for example, when I hear Stan Steiner speaking through the words in his book, *The Vanishing White Man:*

One thing they had learned was this: In the Circle of Life every being is no more or less than any other. "We are all Sisters and Brothers," they said. And so their lives were shared with the "bird, bear, insects, plants, mountains, clouds, stars, sun." To be in harmony with the natural world, one must live within the cycles of life.

Once a wise woman of the Tulalip People, Yesti Blue, who was known as Janet McCloud, told me she thought she knew why the White Man believed in his creation myths. The knowledge of the Circle of Life had been lost to him; he was afraid he was going to die all alone. She told me: "People are like a tree. The leaves of the tree are our thoughts, the branches are our limbs, the trunk is our body, the roots are our veins, where our blood flows from the earth. If you cut the root of the tree, it will die. So the People will die, if you cut their roots from the earth."

Sometimes it is difficult to hear other people and see outside yourself when you use only your ears and not your heart. For example, it's harder to understand people we don't like when we won't allow ourselves to really listen to who they are, try to see why they have to act the way they do with us. I find that when I can totally listen and allow myself to see such people, it becomes difficult not to like them. When I can suspend my critical judgment and try to understand their ideas and their need, I begin to feel really close to them because I can sense what they are going through and what it's like to be them. At each level of understanding it becomes a genuine emotional involvement, an act of love. Such mutual communion helps people understand that they are valuable. And my clearer sense of the other person also illuminates my own ideas about myself.

Not long ago, I received a poem that was precious to me though it had no material value. I saw it as a unique gift, which came from the heart and was grounded in love. It illustrates why I feel that in our world we need to stop being so intent upon naming and classifying our experiences as though they were each somehow separate and devisable entities.

"can we ever know
the dark recesses of
another's loneliness

would VanGogh have
created more
by quantifying
his own loneliness

can you design a question
to touch mine
or me a response
to touch yours

i hope not
for i like to think
each is special

and bounded only
by our willingness to share."

Van Richards

For me, this poem emphasizes three things. We must learn not to hide from each other. We need somehow to believe in our inherent ability to understand things for ourselves. Beginning to trust ourselves is necessary and possible. We are all of us psychologists in our own right, in that we too have studied our subjective inner feelings and thought about how our behaviors are governed. We are also philosophers, even though without portfolio; we can envision that order can be created out of chaos, that we are a part of something exquisitely beautiful when we allow ourselves to live honestly, even if it is sometimes overwhelming and painful to live at all. As philosophers, we can easily see that our study of loneliness is only a study of ourselves and the natural environment to which we inevitably belong, although we often have trouble accepting it as our own. Loneliness is a specific area in the geography of life. It is at the core of all human experience; rather than viewing it as alien territory I believe locating its presence is important for it can be our guide and teacher on our journey through life.

FIVE

PORTRAITS IN LONELINESS

"'When I'm alone'—the words tripped off
  his tongue
As though to be alone were nothing strange.
"'When I was young,' he said. "'When I was
  young. . . .'"
I thought of age, and loneliness, and change.
I thought how strange we grow when we're
  alone,
And how unlike selves that meet and talk,
And blow the candles out, and say good night.
Alone. . . the word is life endured and known.
It is the stillness where our spirits walk
and all but inmost faith is overthrown.'"

                                    Siegfried Sasson

AS people of the "real" world we are often unaware how
close we come each day of our lives to that other very real
world of lonely, desperate people, like the author of this
poem which was handed to me.

  "Two veins
  One idea
  a
  Scream
  That will
  not come.
  Two eyes
  pleading
  blood

> *leap*
> *at*
> *the wrist.*
> *One thought*
> *Love me*
> *dripping on*
> *the floor. . . ."*

The bone-chilling reality of this poem left me with an anger and sadness at the same time. It reopened my feelings about how a depressed person such as the writer of this poem is often observed by members of whatever psychiatric team might have been assembled to assess the motives behind her quiet acts of desperation. My experience leads me to guess that nowhere in their final report will the word "loneliness" ever appear, and yet I feel that when you look behind her words it must have been a factor permeating her life. Her sense of isolation stands out as she tries to communicate, cannot, and then feels unable to control her relationships. Sensing her loss of closeness and understanding with others, she finally makes one last, futile attempt to express the idea that loneliness can seem worse than death.

Clinical teams did most often evaluate emotional problems by psychiatric theories. Psychiatry, a fragile science at best, has no clinical category of *loneliness;* therefore such "symptoms" get jig-sawed into some other diagnosis for which there is a category. (My impression of this has bias, due to my participation over the years in just such clinical group evaluations of people problems.) "Treatment" plans are then built around the diagnosis. The helping professions understand their medical diagnostic terminology too well, and loneliness not well enough.

As I approach middle age, some of the people I care most about are confronting a medical mind-set about their problems of age and its special lonely elements.

I am one of those seemingly-rare people who is utterly in

love with his mother-in-law. "What's wrong with you?" you might be saying. "Nobody in their right mind would admit something as unAmerican as mother-in-law love. But it's delightfully true, and I feel that my mother-in-law and I have an unspoken mutual admiration that gives us a deep and rewarding relationship. During these later years of her life her words seem very touching to me. When I did a taped interview with her, she was in a nursing home in Pennsylvania. She had lost her husband when my wife was very young, and she had brought up her family of four children pretty much alone. Obviously I liked her kids because I married one, and another, her youngest son, was my childhood hero.

She had been a housewife all her life, very active and outgoing, and here she was now in a "home," knowing it was for the rest of her life. She was trying to reconcile her conflicting feelings, viewing herself at age eighty-eight a burden to her children, resenting her limited mobility and her increasing bindness. She is aware that her once beautiful mind drifts at times and that her body is breaking down. And she tried to help me understand her conflicting views on age and loneliness.

"Way back I suppose as a child, I was lonely, but not in my adult life. I guess every child is lonely at times. It doesn't stand out. It isn't a thing I've carried into my adult life, but I think I do get lonely here, but I fight it because I feel it's the best that can be done, and I don't want to worry my family, but it isn't possible to live that well in a nursing home, even though you know two or three nice people, and there's only two or three that I know. But I do have days. Like yesterday I had a day when I was frustrated. Not frustrated, well, just kind of lonely, so I just lay down on my bed and relaxed.

"But, I'm very much blessed, because you see, after my husband died, I had periods of being depressed and lonely, naturally, but I had the four children, and I had Arthur's friendship, and I had Roberta's friendship, and again I was very, very lonely. Yet loneliness is not really a significant part of my life. I guess a great many people that you've interviewed do have periods of loneliness. . . I think it's a thing to avoid. To even feel sorry for yourself. I think that's a psychological thing. I think that's something that you ought to discourage. You should try to think of the pleasant things that have happened to you in the past. The happiness that you've enjoyed. People around whom you have loved and who love you. People like Dick Price who writes me a card every once in a while with a little loving message on it that cheers me up for weeks, and I won't let anybody throw it away.

"I think there is a difference between aloneness and loneliness. People who feel alone, you might say, are more independent, less dependent on other people. People who are alone are not necessarily lonely people, but they're more independent and alone in their thoughts. Lonely people I think, are more fearful and indulgent and care more about themselves. They require companionship.

"Now, I live alone in this room. I have tried to be pleasant and cordial, but there are so few people here that you can have any mental contact with at all; so I come in here and shut the door. Now, most people keep their doors open. But I can't stand the confusion and the noise and people running up and down. It is distracting to me, so I just come in here and shut the door, and I'm alone, and yet I don't feel what you might call loneliness, because I'm able to distract myself with this "talking book." If I didn't have this, well—you see, I can't knit, I can't write, I can't sew. I can't read. I've had to adjust to all those things, and I've done it with the best grace I have in myself. I can't do anything else. Nobody can help me. The doctor said I won't go totally blind, but I'm very much restricted in my sight. I know that if you suddenly came in here and sat down and didn't talk, I probably wouldn't know it was you. I can't see that plain. I can detect things. I know that's a chair. I can see the birds out the window when they feed.

"My son made that feeder . . . He went to work and copied it. He thought it would be an interesting distraction for me. Yes, he made it himself. I had it put outside my window, they gave me permission to have it there, and when it has birdfeed in it, the birds are just flitting back and forth all the time. I don't get anything interesting . . . the Cardinals, as you know, don't like that kind of food. They're awful fussy. They like only sunflower seeds. I hear them all around me, but they don't come to my feeder."

You know, I've been feeling the significance of those birds for "Gram" as she lives there in her personal and lonely space. This opened for me many feelings about how our histories had interrelated since I was a boy of seven and first knew her. There is so much looking back at any age, and yet the quality of her looking back sustained her now, because she could dwell on the positive aspects of it. It wasn't morbid—she had managed to assess her life and value it without overly dwelling on the negative and letting it totally defeat her. She was managing. I see this as true in my own life, for whatever experiences I have had, good and bad, they are enormously valuable to me now. I tried to recapture that in the following story I wrote and sent to her shortly after we had done this interview. I was dealing with a sense of what I call "nostalgia loneliness"— for something that once was and can never be again, and yet, its effect is present in the now.

Did I Ever Tell You?

I guess I thought you'd never ask. No one has before. I always said that if anybody should ever ask me, I'd have to say it right out loud. I've have to say, "Yes, I am in love-with mango jelly, that is."

To be in love with a mango jelly seems funny to you, I'll bet. But then, you didn't know Nancy Allen either!

And I bet you never heard of Spoon Hollins, the cartoon character, either. Spoon Hollins?

Nancy Allen's father was the cartoonist who created Spoon Hollins for the comic strips.

That was a long time ago. We were just kids. Nancy was all tanned and nice looking and pretended she didn't like me much. It was only her girlfriends in school who kept letting me know how she really felt, just like my friends would let it slip that I was stuck on her.

We always acted uninterested, but somehow we always did things together, like grab something personal the other had and run off, knowing we'd be chased. That was how I touched her breast one time by mistake. We ran so hard she fell down, and I sprawled over her, landing with my outstretched arm on her. Naturally, we pretended it hadn't happened, but it had. And yet, how come after all these years, I'm still in love with her, and me married to someone else and all that?

I say I'm in love with Nancy Allen! Yet, I was only twelve years old when I lived in Sarasota, Florida. Still you can fall in love at twelve.

I suppose you're going to say, how come she doesn't even know I'm in love with her? I suppose you'll ask a question like that. Like, how come, if I loved her so much, I never said it to her face?

Well, her father was the Fred Allen, the cartoonist, and he had his own office over the store. In fact, everyone in his family was a genius, even Nancy. They invented Tree-Ripe Mango Jelly and they sold it to people in West Florida. Can you imagine a family that talented? The year I had to move back to Scranton, Pennsylvania, Nancy made a beautiful clay sculpture ten inches high, of a nude woman standing next to a stump. I didn't know that she had made it for me exactly, since she exhibited it first in the Out-of-Door School Art Show, but, just before I had to go, she ran up and gave me this big box all wrapped in brown paper and said not to open it until later.

I never told her I loved her, but I know she knew. When I got up North, I put the statue in a big can and buried it in the soft dirt hillside of our back yard, so my parents wouldn't see it. It was a beautiful nude. Sometimes I dug it up, just to look at it. I yell ya, I was heartbroken when I came back from the war and never could find the spot where I had hidden it. It's there now, somewhere, only I don't live in Scranton and I don't own the property. Some day, if I make a lot of money, I'm going to buy our old place back and dig up that whole hillside until I find my nude.

I eat mango jelly almost every morning, I always have, maybe I always will. I can't get Tree-Ripe Mango Jelly any more, so I buy Smuckers—"With a name like that, it's got to be pretty good."

So, now you know my secret—and probably my deepest secret. I'm in love with Nancy Allen! You know, I haven't seen her since then, either. Maybe she's dead. To her I was a hero, I think. I'll never know for sure.

Sometimes it makes me lonely to think of her, and her friend, Holly Carter, too. I loved them both I think. Maybe some time I'll try to write to her—to both of them because their identities run together in my remembering. Maybe I'll just write in care of the Tree-Ripe Mango Jelly Company, Sarasota, Florida.

★ ★ ★

I would like to use the writing of this story to demonstrate a point. When we are feeling nostalgic like this, or even depressed, lonely, or just bored, it is as though there is an emptiness in us that we can't fathom. The question is, how do we get a handle on it?

One way is to reach out to someone else.

When I wrote to Gram, I sent the story along to cheer her up, but I also wrote because I needed to express thoughts buried within me; her pain made me feel very close to her, and it touched something deep in me. I needed to use the story medium as though it was a personal journey to clarify something for myself that I was only half aware of. Perhaps without fully knowing why, I felt that any affirmative action was better than no action. As I began to write, I spontaneously filled in the blank spaces and came away with clearer feelings, which extended to Gram, to people whom I had loved; even better, when I had finished, I felt a sense of completion and a new thrust to tell other people around me how important they also were.

I am sure that Gram appreciated my sending her this little story because, lurking inside her stoic exterior lies a seldom-touched and hidden romantic who has trouble putting this part of herself into words. I think a lot of people are this way.

Gram's experience illustrates lonely feelings which are mostly the result of a specific situation. The degree and quality of her feelings, however, are not determined by the nursing home. The nursing home does not *make* her lonely, any more than an abusive word can *make* us feel bad unless we give credence to that word. No, the character and definition of Gram's feelings are determined by how she herself perceives and reacts to her surroundings.

Another type of loneliness is illustrated by Jodie Warren -

I can't help thinking of her just now. A short time ago I sent her a message on tape along with another of the stories that I had written. Jodie is a frail, bright, twenty-three year old single woman, who has just made the difficult decision to leave home to live in an "alternative living" complex with ten other handicapped adults. Jodie is increasingly confined to a wheelchair with a form of severe congenital paralysis, which leaves her with almost no mobility. Quite unexpectedly, Jodie and I discovered that we have a natural attraction for each other. It expressed itself like this, in a letter I received:

"Dear Dick,

I'm sending you a copy of the paper
on loneliness I did at your suggestion.
As I said in the paper, it does seem
strange that you sent me that tape now
instead of a few years ago, when I was
so desperate for help. I feel that I
should admit that the reason that I
joined the National Square Rigger Society
⟋an educational-marine program I am
involved with as an avocation⟋ was that
after reading about you in the paper, I
wanted to make contact with you. I
remember you said something about
loneliness that really hit me. I didn't
quite dare to write you then . .

Peace, Jodie"

LONELINESS

I speak first in answer to the question, "Have you
ever been lonely?" The question seems sadly laugh-
able now, because I spent so many desperate years
trapped in a tiny cage of fear and loneliness. If it had
been asked a couple of years ago, I would have been
overjoyed at the chance to finally communicate. For
the real futility of loneliness is the inability to communicate.

In some ways I think the worst is over, since I now
have lots of people I can communicate with. But
sometimes it comes to me clearly that the worst is still
ahead. At these moments, I am haunted by the specter
of the living corpse I may become. Other people with
the disease I have end their days blind, deaf, shriveled
things; unable to move, unable to talk; unable to cry.
The loneliness such a being must feel is unimagin-
able.

Still, I think that the really acute pain of my experiences with loneliness and depression are the result of
not talking to people about my fears for the future. I

think no one is strong enough to face such a tragic probability alone, and it is absurd that I expected it of myself. Having that support now, I realize more clearly what it was that I needed so desperately for so many years.

Loss of loved ones brings another special type of loneliness. And I have had to adjust to this painful situation as well as my own disability. From the moment my father died suddenly during the dreadful cold and storms last January, life became even more traumatic for my mother and me. What followed was a melange: the frantic long-distance phone calls, the days of hub-bub and cheer of friends and relatives, the bleakness of the occasion. I remember the poignancy of the loneliness I felt when we came home from the funeral, having said good-bye to the friends and relatives. We came home to our empty house and to the realization that it would always be empty. This loneliness lurks still in the shadows of our house; it sometimes reaches out to claw at us as we sit at the dinner table and notice the empty place.

I know this is no original discovery, but I have found that a good remedy for loneliness is to involve yourself in the problems of someone else. In the last few years I have been fortunate enough to know several people who have even more troubles than I have. Talking to them about their problems, sharing their fears and frustrations, brings comfort and rewards. One of these rewards is understanding feelings of loneliness and isolation, by learning that other people have them, too.

Jodie's acute form of loneliness has largely been affected by the chronic physical situation she endures. She maintains her outgoing perspective by having come to grips with the fact that, like all of us, she is alone in many ways, which only she can accept and manage. Instead of losing her sense of self-esteem and emotional control, she has gained something enormously beautiful—the ability to accept what *is*.

★ ★ ★

Not everyone deals effectively with loneliness; Jim Crane has not mastered his tribulations.

Jim's story seems to me to be one of defeat. He too, is only twenty-three, but the feelings he is experiencing at this time are not related to any specific traumatic situation in his life. They are long-standing feelings, which stem from his perception of a whole series of small defeats, which leave him believing himself to be unattractive, powerless and alone.

> *"Where was everyone yesterday, or did I run away? Was everyone with each other? Like I was with me? Did I hear them call to me and not turn around? I am the Game player, I toss the dice. The game I play is "loser." I sit in the dealer's chair, in my empty room. I play a game called Loneliness, and I hold all the hands."*

There is no hero image pictured here. The principal characteristic of a "hero" is courage. But Jim's mirror image is one of failure. Physically he is a well-built American male, but his lack of self-confidence makes him more a handicapped prisoner than my friend Jodie, in her wheelchair.

Jim imagines, as lonely people so often do, that everyone else is finding success in their quest for caring and closeness. At this point he is afraid to try.

Perhaps he is not aware of other lonely scenes that repeat themselves so often in different parts of his own home town. Other lonely people are hiding, too, but in different ways, behind their self-confidence masks.

Don and Cathy wear two of these masks.

You might meet them late at night if you enter one of the better local hotel night clubs or after-dinner spots. Many of the early evening diners have left for the theater or the movies or home. The crowd is different now that it's well past 11:00 p.m., a little louder than before and more a mix of young and old. A few women arrive together in small groups, most of the people are single. It's a scene repeated in many of the hotels, bars, and late-night "watering holes" around the city, any city in America. Closing time in this particular place is earlier than most, and there is an atmosphere of activity as people move from the bar stools or tables to circulate and then return, either alone or in pairs. It is the midnight "coupling-place" in full swing, and time is running out for the losers in the game. A man in his mid-forties stands at the far corner of the bar holding his drink. He seems less hesitant than some of the others. Finally, after ordering another drink, he picks up his glass and moves into the crowd milling noisily about.

"Hi, I'm Don."

"I'm Cathy."

"Hi, Cathy, been here before?"

"Are you kidding? I don't come to these places much."

"Me, neither."

"Well, I didn't think I'd seen you around."

"Well, I haven't seen you either."

"Having fun?"

"Well . . ."

"How about us, then Cathy? Cathy, do you want to?"

"Want to?"

"Fuck."

"That's crude! I don't like that kind of talk—what do you think I am anyway?"

"Do you want to?"

"I said you shouldn't say things like that!"

"It's getting late; besides, I like you."

"Well, I don't like people to use words like that with me. That bothers me."

"I'm sorry, but Cathy, do you want?"

"Do I want to what?"

"Sleep with me. You turn me on."

"Well, it's too crude to approach a person like that. It's too fast."

"Cathy, it's almost one o'clock in the morning. I'd really

like to get to know you better. What do you say we get out of here together. I'd like that."

"Why don't we just have a drink together, huh?"

"Cathy, I like you, I want to be with you tonight."

"Well, you are with me now. Let's just have a drink and see."

"Let's get out of here, be together."

"One drink first, O.K.?"

"Cathy!"

"Let's just not go so fast."

"O.K., one drink!"

"One drink."

"But no more, O.K.?"

"O.K."

"Then we'll go?"

"We'll go."

Loneliness like the conversation of Don and Cathy can be repetitive, a needle stuck in a familiar nicked record's groove or it can strike new chords. Another instance of loneliness is that of Janet Conway.

Janet Conrad is special to me. She has a rare beauty that just seems to shine out from the strength of her spiritual belief and her honesty. I recognized this within the first moments of meeting her at the hospital bedside of a mutual friend who was dying of cancer. We have shared a lot together since that time and she typifies for me the role that courage and religious convictions can play in the management of loneliness for many people.

It has been six years since Janet's husband suddenly found "another woman" and walked away from his wife and three children.

". . . I've said that it was like having your skin stripped off, but it really happened and I have come to this rockbottom place a lot of times where I don't have any support except from me and God. That's the bottom line!

"It is not such a bad thing, you know, because that is, in fact, where we're headed, I believe. Getting to know me and getting to be comfortable with myself, is a new experience. I have time to think.

"I still have a horrid time with trust, though. One night not too long ago I had a really scary experience, and I think it had something to do with my loneliness. A few nights previously I had received an obscene phone call, which is really kind of scary because you don't know whether they are just dialing randomly or if they know who you are and where you are.

"Then a few nights later, I had gone to sleep about midnight and I woke to hear the bell ring, I thought. I sat bolt upright, wide awake, and I thought someone was at my door in the middle of the night. So, I put on my robe and went to the door. By this time I was shaking all over. I was sure it was the doorbell, you know, but it was not. I checked the furnace, checked the kids, tucked everybody in. When I got back to my bedroom I just got down on my knees and read the Scriptures for ten or fifteen minutes.

"I had been feeling this kind of radical aloneness, where there isn't really anybody else here but me and these kids. Maybe that's something you keep under wraps because that kind of responsibility is kind of scary to look at too. . .

"I used to do a pretty good job of hiding how I felt inside. I put up defenses. But at the same time I had this habit of judging myself very harshly, then I would feel guilty.

"Not long after the doorbell incident an amazing thing happened. I was watching the sunset one night. I was praying for the ability to let go of whatever it was that was blocking me from experiencing myself as a whole person, loved by God, and so forth.

"I was thinking this had a lot to do with my earlier experiences, not forgiving my mother specifically, not forgiving my husbnd, and not forgiving myself.

"At that moment I had the feeling of someone saying to me 'I look at you as a gentle friend would look at you.' In other words, it was like the Lord saying, 'I am your gentle friend. How would a person who really cares about and who was really going to judge you and perceive you in the most friendly, kind, gentle way look at your life? How would that person view who you are and what you do? That's how I want you to look at yourself. That is, in fact, how I look at you.'

"Suddenly, I had a feeling of such peace, I started to cry. I knew all at once that God wasn't the problem. My perceiving was the problem . . . I had such a feeling of gentleness and compassion for myself. It was like looking at myself objectively, from outside and saying 'This person has had a bad time. You must be very gentle with her.'

"This was really good, because I think a neurotic kind of thing is always to look at a thousand potentially positive things, see one negative thing, and worry about it, and worry about it, until you lose complete sight of all the positives. It's what lonely people do so much. It is what I always did myself.

"I'm beginning to accept a little better that there is darkness, there is light, and there is shadow, also, to things in my life. The only way I'll be able to change these things is first to accept them. . . ."

That is an enormously beautiful statement Janet made to me. I especially treasure Janet's words when I am feeling alone or unsure and I need to reconnect with that pure essence of spiritual belief that is available to each of us. I believe that in those moments when Janet made her own connection she found what mystics of many faiths have called "the divine within," and what Meister Eckhardt meant when he wrote, "The Eye with which I see God is the Eye with which God sees me."

Janet's faith has come from within, sustained her, and she is gradually forgiving herself.

★ ★ ★

For some people honesty is the beginning of self-forgiveness. Harold is one such person:

My friend Harold carries just 135 pounds on a 6'4"

frame. At one time we had talked together about some problem he was having. During the weeks in which we were preparing to discontinue our work together we talked a lot about what our not being with each other would mean. He was able to talk about his somewhat chronic sense of isolation and about his feelings of being left behind. He knew that I was working on this project and wanted to help. Shortly after I left the agency, he sent me this note.

"Hi . . .

"I'm writing this to you to try to explain what my loneliness is like. I come home from work to find nobody here, and can feel the emptiness. I understand that my mother is at my widowed brother's house, and she is helping him with the kids, but I still feel alone.

"This feeling of being lonely is unusual because it is a feeling I have had my entire life but never knew what it was until I went into psychotherapy. I've never been much of a mixer with people, and in fact, usually stayed away from getting close to anyone.

"Though I've always had a fear of death, there were times when I wanted to die. I passed my twentieth and thirtieth birthdays without any trouble. Then, on my fortieth birthday, I suddenly felt old and scared and more lonely than ever. Sometimes when I am in bed at night, I have weird dreams. I will dream that my mother has died and I am not able to adjust to being without her.

"Sometimes I will be lonely and get nervous, so I will get something to eat. Eating at times like this is something I have done almost my whole life. But don't get me wrong. Sometimes I eat because I just enjoy eating.

"Loneliness is being in bed at night and being unable to hear my mother breathing in the next room, and getting up and seeing the blanket rising up and down, and then feeling okay. Also, being alone at night while watching TV, and finding myself carrying on a monologue with a member of my family or someone at work, or with my counselor. I am fine talking one-on-one with anyone, but if I am in a conversation with more than one person, I become self-conscious and have trouble knowing what to say.

"One thing out of the ordinary has happened these past several days. I have been able to concentrate more on reading my paper and watching TV and I have felt less lonely. Consequently, I have had a tough time in writing down my thoughts on loneliness. I thought for a week about what to write, and it has taken me two days to do the writing. I hope this letter will help you to help me.

Respectfully,
Harold."

I have seen Harold once or twice since those years we worked together and it feels good to see him. There's always a bear hug and a genuine sense of pleasure in store. He typifies for me the potential we have for reversing the destructive sense of confusion that often accompanies extreme loneliness or feelings of differentness.

In the intervening time Harold has been able to look at himself more honestly. This has changed his perception of himself. When you change your perception, you've inevitably changed your behavior, too. When you modify behavior, feelings change. Harold is moving from a faulty set of behaviors that were not paying off, to new altered behaviors, and a better self-image.

★ ★ ★

One person who feels unable to cope with her enrivon- ment I call "The Woman Who Sits Alone." Sometimes she says, "I love you but not right now! You make me angry because you make me face myself." She has another name of course, but this one fits. She is an attractive, very gifted forty-six-year-old divorced woman with four teenaged children at home, and she hungers for male companion- ship, but is so afraid no one will ever care for her again that she effectively removes herself from any opportunities to be close with men.

I remember that we sat together in a public meeting at the library one time and she suddenly leaned over to me and whispered, "Have you ever been lonely?" "Yes," I answered jokingly, "and each time I thought it would be my last."

Then she leaned over again and whispered, "What do you do, when you get lonely?" I whispered back the only thing that came to me at that odd moment. "Well," I said, "I learned something of value from a friend of mine. I bor- rowed it from her' maybe it will be useful to you, too. Ask yourself this question, say:

'Mirror, mirror of my mind
I look inside and what do I find?'

She looked at me quizzically, then whispered, "I see nothing." "Look again," I encouraged. "Loneliness," she said at last, sucking in her breath, and speaking more to herself than to me, "and how I avoid seeing it." "But, loneliness *is* something!" I explained. "Loneliness is something you are living, it's part of life, look deeper."

By now we were both engrossed in our whispered com- munications and the meeting we were attending droned on without us.

"Well, I see myself in my car, alone as usual, or at home, feeling alone as usual, at work, alone but wishing I could let myself be closer to people around me. I'm an avoider!" "Stay with the mirror image," I suggested, "and then let's talk again after a bit."

I went home that night thinking about this charming, lonely woman. I felt compelled to write this short description and I gave it to her the next time we met.

". . . A woman sits alone, her car parked amid others on a dusty, wind-honed parking lot. There is no sage brush or cactus growing in this typical American desert.

She has been here before—every day, to be exact. She has chosen this time to come because it is halfway in the endless hours between breakfast and dinner. She comes because sitting by herself in her car, hear other people, seems more bearable than loneliness alone. She does not know what we know. Nor has she yet discovered, through the magic of telephone, the soothing, friendly voice on the weather report answering tape.

And tonight, while she struggles to find peace in sleep, lovers somewhere will contemplate a promise of new moonlight."

I didn't see her for a number of weeks after that, but when I did, she took me aside and handed me this poem she had written. "Your description is right," she said. "Only it didn't go far enough."

It's 3 a.m. and sultry, the boys are restless on Main,
I hear them out there once again tonight.
The wild young men of summer are racing in the
    darkness,
And standing on their unforgiving brakes.

They split the air with screechings.
The noise is harsh and frightening,
They're burning out their engines and their minds.

I bolted out of sleep just now,
Wondering if they'd smash it all this time.
Would they toss up bloody on my doorstep.
Would they find the desperate end they seek?
Have they no better worlds to conquer?
Would fifty girls not soothe their inner rage?

I toss and turn and worry sadly;
I cannot understand such alien ways.
And Yet—in sleepless fantasy I wander;
I wish myself a hundred miles away,
Awakened in some inn beside the ocean,
Listening to the pounding surf outside.

And if some gentle stranger slept beside me,
I do not think I'd even ask his name.
It makes me laugh in quiet desperation;
The boys and I each play a lonely game."

Another lonely person I know is Barbara Wells.

When I first interviewed Barbara Wells, she was fifty-six and living alone. She felt that life had treated her badly since the time her husband had died some years ago. Because of her loneliness the vision of her life had changed, she seldom looked at herself as anything but a loser now. It was hard for her to remember her strengths—or the joy of a crisp morning.

In many ways, her loneliness has its origin in her childhood, when she felt isolated and unappreciated by parents who were able to give her only limited affection and caring. She had married Bill "to get away" from a poor home situation and from feelings of inadequacy and aloneness.

We sat together for several hours one evening talking about her loneliness. She summed up some of it like this:

"... It will soon be eight years since Bill died, and for a whole year I didn't go anywhere as far as any social activities went, and then I started. Unfortunately, I started the bottle move for company. I just wanted to be with people ... I'd go down to the Crystal Palace and I'd sit in the furthest corner. I had my little spot and the waitress knew I bought my own drinks and all that bit, but you know, a gal alone in a bar room is still not in the greatest spot to be. And I knew it, but it didn't concern me because I figured I'm lonely, and I'd watch, you know. Well, I knew the girl who plays the organ there, she had been a friend of Bill's and mine. Well, she called me about a year later and she said, 'What are you doing?' And I said, 'Not a thing.' So she said, 'Well, why don't you get dressed and come down. I'll see that you get a ride home.' Which was the way that it went. You know.

"And then I started to blossom out and go to the Palace. I had gone to the Palace for years to eat lunch and whatever, but I never went into the cocktail lounge alone. But it got so I, you know, I had a few fellows that I was seeing here and there and whatever. Nobody that I got emotionally involved with at all, but I was looking, looking, looking for someone to care about me again. I know it seems kind of ridiculous, but I was like a little kid.

"See, I met Bill when I was sixteen, and I married him when I was eighteen, so I really never had any, you know, the boyfriend bit. I had a crush on a couple of fellows when I was fourteen, fifteen, holding hands and going to the movies when my father wasn't looking.

"But I never really had a relationship to go out and sort of test, see, 'Do I like this one, do I like that one?' And I sort of went through it in my old blind, drinking way, and then I met one fellow, almost the first couple of months that I went out. In fact, my friend down at the lounge, the organist, introduced me to him, and for four or five years, he was in and out of my life like a yo-yo. Unfortunately, we did a lot of drinking together. He'd come by for a while, and then all of a sudden, I wouldn't hear from him for six, eight, ten months, he'd take off for California or something. That's the history, and unfortunately, I became emotionally involved with him. I cared about him. I knew there wasn't any future in it, and I had a great deal of guilt about it, and I was just as lonely with him as I was without him, really.

"I was never not lonely, even when he'd come by and he loved to cook, and I would shop, and we'd put the meals on and I'd clean up. I wasn't keeping my house like I should. It was cluttered to an extreme. That bothered me, and I didn't know where to begin.

I'd make sort of stabbing attempts at straightening things out. I went through periods for a long time. It just wasn't normal. I know it, Dick. I have to face it.

". . . Well, I got so tired of seeing him sit there with his hands cupped and watching my black and white TV and complaining because I didn't have a colored one working. And it was a big nothing, and finally one day I just said, 'I'm not seeing you any more. You're not coming over.' He'd bring up chop suey and he'd bring this bottle, but he'd close the bars first and then he'd come by, right? So I finally got the cobwebs straightened out enough to decide I wasn't that lonely. And I wasn't used to being treated shabbily. My husband treated me like a queen, you know.

"For a while I saw another fellow in town until I found out he was married, and I just didn't see him anymore, because that's one thing I did not do was mess around with married fellows. I was lonely, but I figured there were fellows around that were lonely and not married. Then a fellow in town called me. The last time he called me was maybe a year ago, and he was a policeman, a detective, and he just couldn't understand why I didn't want to see him. But I just told him that I didn't want to see him because he was married. Well, he told me he was married and separated, and they were divorcing. I called up one day and he answered the phone, but he was very, very angry. 'Don't ever call this number again!' So that's when I saw the light. And I was sort of fond of him. I was still lonely, though, because I knew he didn't care about me, and he didn't. . . .

"I found out that the life I was leading didn't work; it wasn't great and it was pretty dangerous. All the fellows I met, you know, the fellows would line up at the bar and they'd look you over, and I felt like I was on display. I really resented it. And I didn't like it when somebody came up and asked me to dance and then the first thing they wanted to know was if they could take you home and have a six-pack or something. It was always some little cheapie thing, you know.

"I really got very, very resentful, and I was trying very definitely to bring myself up, not pull myself down any more; and so I didn't need this. So I'd go maybe once or twice, then I wouldn't go again, and it wasn't that I felt better than anyone else there. I just didn't feel as though I belonged. I couldn't find a little niche that I felt happy or content with. . . I haven't gotten beyond that point, Dick, where I think, you know, like some fairy prince, a great big wonderful guy, is going to come riding by on a big white horse and swoop me up and make me happy for the rest of my life. I don't feel that any more. . . ."

As in so many cases, loneliness is a struggle between dependence and independence. Barbara longed for a miraculous happening, something permanent that she could hold onto, but she forgot her own peace of mind in the helter-skelter tactics to alleviate her loneliness. She was afraid to be alone or to allow herself to recognize her own strengths. She feared the loss of her identity and authenticity because originally she had believed that without a man she was only half a person. That's the way she often referred to herself, "I'm half a person, he didn't leave me with much." Her lonely feelings stemmed from many experiences in her life and just seemed to grow until she now felt continually alone and without any resources of her own. She had trouble adapting to her changing situation when Bill died and she began to use alcohol to soothe her feelings and give her at least the momentary illusion of strength. It didn't work. In spite of her very real potential for happiness, Barbara continues to avoid the responsibilities inherent in close relationships. I feel that she continues to deceive herself as well as her friends.

I don't place such importance, as others seem to, on distinguishing between the five words "loneliness," "aloneness," "solitude," "alienation," and "isolation," as a way of understanding the felt experience of loneliness. However, word definitions do offer a way of separating out and portraying our feelings, and therefore, they can aid us in learning how to apply the word *Loneliness* to our lives. Certainly as far as understanding the experience of loneliness goes, these words have a degree of interchangeability.

The various forms of loneliness have never been clearly conceptualized and distinguished, and because of its highly-personal and subjective nature the one defining word "loneliness" has had to do double and triple duty at times. Compare, for example, the loneliness of a little boy who is confined to bed for a day without Mom being around, with the loneliness of the woman whose long-time lover has just left her. "Loneliness" fails to capture the distinguishing features between these two obviously different experiences and yet both are feeling "loneliness."

I believe that within the root meaning of each of the five words is a single unifying influence which relates in one way or another to the fear of being alone. There are a few basic clarifiers that we might use to understand the interrelatedness of each of these words and I will try to characterize them here:

"Loneliness" refers to the subjective personal feeling (real or imagined) of being not related, not meaningfully connected, alone, being alone in the world. There is something sad about the sense of void that we are aware of in loneliness. It is consciously experienced with some degree of pain, sometimes slight, at other times overwhelming. Generally, loneliness involves internal and external conditions. It is a universal and ultimate condition. It is an unwanted feeling of estrangement from the world, from the self or from others. Although loneliness is a private experience, it reflects in some way upon the reality of our social environment. Loneliness usually includes a sense of loss of control over the situation. The intensity of the experience depends upon the nature of the feelings involved. You do not have to be alone to be lonely.

"Marriage can be lonely. Mine was. We shared the same roof, our son, household chores. We did not share goals, feelings, ourselves. I know room mates who are closer than we were . . . The loneliness I felt when we were together was as if I were being pushed by heavy weights into a quagmire out of which there was no escape . . . I had gilded the lily by convincing myself that being with someone else would ease that pain in my chest . . . 'Loneliness' is a most self-centered activity . . . I only become afraid when there is no one close."

Carol Brill

"Loneliness. . . . It means not having anyone around. It means being out in the cold, being rejected, being—to me, being pregnant only don't be looking for an inn, with no place to put a baby. You know, it's having a need for something and not having a way of getting that done, and nobody cares."

Julie Smith

"Aloneness" (or *"alone"*) meaning to be by oneself, generally refers to an objective state as opposed to the subjective state of loneliness. An example might be "I went off on a hillside just to be by myself." Often aloneness can be visibly observed. This is not true of loneliness. "Aloneness" doesn't have to be negatively experienced. You can "live alone and like it."

You're not bothered by loneliness when you are alone in a highly-reinforcing situation. The prospector looking for uranium may be alone with only an old mule, but he's not lonely when he's getting hot leads about where the uranium is. Also, he *chose* this aloneness and solitude.

The prospector's possibly productive aloneness contrasts sharply with times of desperate "alone-ness" when no consolation seems possible. Lois Kirk explains how this alienation felt to her:

". . . I was with mother for a short time before she died. She was going through terminal cancer. She and I talked. We both knew she was dying. We didn't say, 'Hey, you're dying.' But we both knew what the situation was. The last time I saw her, she was in the hospital and the doctors knew she wouldn't be coming home. I didn't really want to leave, but I had flown out to see her. I had a few days between exams here and there was just sort of an understanding between us, and she knew, finally, I was on my way. But up to this time in a sense, she had been supporting me in a way, taking care of me in a way, giving me strength. And to me it was almost as though she said to me, 'Hey, I know you're on your way, now. It's O.K. to let go.' And I really felt that way. The last thing she said to me was, 'You've got to go, Lois.' And I answered, 'I've got to go, Mom.' And she said, 'That's right, you've got a big job to take care of. You do it.' So, she knew and I knew. And it's hard. But there's not a loneliness, exactly. I don't quite know how to describe it to you. There was no one who could have touched me at that time, who could have comforted me or anything else. But that's what I mean about the difference between being alone and loneliness. When I'm lonely, a person can comfort me. When I'm alone, no one can comfort me."

Lois was in pain. Being alone, like aloneness, can promote negative or positive feelings, depending on how we experience it, but the distinguishing factor between these two and loneliness is that in loneliness, there is *always* some degree of pain.

"I'm fascinated with old headstones. The names and all the little babies. Everybody died so young. I love that. When my husband was alive, I used to make him stop up in New Hampshire and Vermont and everywhere, and just go into old cemeteries, you know, and just wander about—people and their lives. So I did that myself and I walked and walked and walked, and it is very lonely. . . . after he died. I walked through the cemetery where he was buried. His grave was all covered with snow and the little wall just showing and I thought about my husband so much all the time we were being buried with the storm. I thought, 'He's down there, and he's cold and he's alone.' But he really isn't hurting, you know. Is it normal to think that way? It's hard to let people go. It's terribly hard. I've had two whole years, you know, of being alone and I don't resent it. It's just that I'm still saying WHY?"

Louise Randall

I think many of the people I'm writing about feel miserable about themselves at times. My guess is that people who feel miserable about themselves are going to feel lonely because it will be hard for them to feel acceptable or connected while they are in that mood. Often they can't feel accepted, because they have a special mind set about how bad it is to be feeling lonely and they're not ready to be accepted. If you're not ready to be accepted, you can feel pretty damn lonely. It's a vicious circle, isn't it, because it can just reinforce that feeling that there's something wrong with you.

Maureen's story may illustrate this for you.

"... Well, it seems to me, I've had a very inadequate feeling as I said, all my life, but I also felt like I just didn't belong anywhere. There wasn't a niche where I could, you know, really find a spot and be comfortable, and with my husband, I was comfortable. He was sort of overprotecting, you know, ... then, all of a sudden he left me and just wasn't there any more. I used to wake up in the morning and I'd feel like a grown woman, you know, like I was fifty-one, and still I'd feel like I can't face the day. I can't cope with it, and I would be frightened of things that I used to do even when he was with me. You know, it was like I'd just wake up in the morning, and I wanted to stay in that bed and go to sleep and not even face life. To me it was ridiculous, but there it was and it took me a great long time to overcome it—I probably never will, completely."

"*Solitude*" and loneliness are often used together but they are not the same. Solitude mostly carries with it positive connotations, although it can also be a negative. Sometimes we seek solitude but we never seek loneliness. Solitude is a state of being or living alone. Often we feel that we can find creativity, joy and peace in solitude; so it may be viewed as an enriching inner experience and doesn't necessarily depend on our being isolated or alone. I need to suggest, however, that solitude always leads us to the same place, an appreciation of non-aloneness. Solitude with no hope of return to others would be intolerable. So, solitude is only good in relation to something else, it becomes a relative thing.

> ". . . . There's a lot more alone-time things I'd like to do. I don't get away by myself very often and when I do, I thoroughly enjoy it. My mother has a cottage on a lake in the middle of nowhere. . . . I spent a week there in the fall and it was absolutely gorgeous. The rain and I were friends. The firelight and I were friends. It was just a gorgeous week. When I get off by myself alone for just a day or so like that, then I can meet people with all kinds of new energy."
>
> Simon Toms

"*Isolation*" meaning to be alone or separate from others, can be an objective or subjective term. This differs from loneliness, which in terms of feelings is used only in the subjective sense. "Social isolation" however, meaning not participating with other people. This can bring about feelings of loneliness. In isolation we can be or feel socially or psychologically cut off without physically being separated from other people or things. The distinction has been made that "social isolation" is "*being isolated*" while "psychological isolation" is "*feeling isolated*." It is quite possible that social isolation is the most common experience which brings on loneliness. There is a close connection between loneliness and isolation, however, and often the words are used interchangeably. I feel, at times, it is inaccurate to do this. For example, we can choose to be socially isolated if we wish, and people can observe that in our physical aloneness we have isolated ourselves. We cannot observe the emotional or physical condition of loneliness this same way.

Patricia Martin, age forty, is facing her own sense of isolation when she says:

". . . Yes, I had to have something or somebody around me who was paying attention to me or going some place or doing something. I don't know why I'm like that, I just know it's a part. . . . I think it is a part of ongoing adolescence. When I was younger, I wanted a baby so bad. I thought that was everything—so I could fill in the gap in the loneliness. It was like I was lonely, so for that reason, I got married, and like, if he had to work and I was home, I was still lonely, so I wanted a baby, and I had a baby, and I thought that was great until she got older. Then, when she went to school, I had another one, then she got older and by that time I had an operation and couldn't have any more. So I went to work and that helped a lot. And then my marriage deteriorated. My first husband and I were separated, and then, loneliness again. When he said like . . . he didn't say he didn't love me or he didn't say he did love me—he said he didn't want the responsibility because he wanted to be let free a little bit and that was like a knife going through my heart.

"I still think about it; it still hurts. But I could see what I was doing to him. I was smothering him with my loneliness . . . because I was lonely, I was clinging to him, which was smothering him—like I was smothering my kids. I feel I've got to accept loneliness as a part of my life, to lift up my abilities, to fill the gap every single moment of the day, and if I'm going to be lonely, say, 'Hey, it's just a passing thing, and nobody loves me or wants me, and just because he doesn't live here any more, or the kids aren't here anymore, I don't have to go into deeper despair. I can deal, you know!—but then I wonder where is everybody?"

Patricia Martin

"*Alienation*" is frequently associated with "loneliness." It involves some kind of a separation or a withdrawing. It can be either a subjective feeling or an objective act. We can remove ourself from a group of people and become alienated without feeling lonely, but we can also feel lonely without actually being alienated. "Alienation" generally is not interchangeable with "loneliness," but they are close in meaning. The difference is, "loneliness" is not chosen. Often "alienation" refers to selecting separation from a group, whereas, "loneliness" is unwanted, has pain attached and most often refers to the distress of a concrete individual.

I would like to offer what I think is a haunting and poignant example of the subjective sense of what it is like to feel alienated.

POEM FROM AN ENGLISH CLASS

He always.
He always wanted to explain things.
But no one cared.
So he drew. . . .

Sometimes he would draw and it wasn't anything.
He wanted to carve it in a stone or write it in the sky.
And it would be only the sky and him and the things
inside him that needed saying.
And it was after that he drew the picture.
He kept it under his pillow and let no one see it.
And he would look at it every night and think about it.
And when it was dark and his eyes were closed, he could
still see it.
And it was all of him.

And he loved it.

When he went to school he brought it with him.
Not to show anyone, but just to have it with him, like a
friend.
It was funny about school.
He sat in a square brown desk.
Like all the other square brown desks.
And he thought it should be red.
And his room was a square brown room, like all the
other rooms.

And it was tight and close. And stiff.
He hated to hold the pencil and chalk, with his arms stiff
and his feet flat on the floor.
STIFF.
With the teacher watching and waiting.

The teacher came and spoke to him.
She told him to wear a tie like all the other boys.
He said he didn't like them.
She said that it didn't matter.
And after that they drew.
And he drew all yellow and that was the way he felt
about the morning. And it was beautiful.
The teacher came and smiled at him.
"What's this?" she said. "Why don't you draw somthing
like Ken is drawing?"
"Isn't that beautiful?"

After that his mother bought him a tie.
And he always drew airplanes and rocketships like
everyone else.
And he threw the old picture away.

And when he lay alone looking at the sky it was big and
blue and all of everything. But he wasn't anymore.
He was square inside and brown.
And his hands were stiff and he was like everyone else.
And all the things inside him that needed saying didn't
need it anymore.
It had stopped pushing.
It was crushed.
STIFF.
Like everything else.

(This poem was given to a grade 12 English teacher in a California school. Two weeks later, the student committed suicide.)

What troubles me about all the loneliness-connected definitions in the dictionaries and textbooks is that there is an implication that they are each pure, and they're not. There's a fuzziness when you talk about loneliness. It's not that easy trying to box in these word definitions like so many statistical units on a graph, where you look at the high point of the graph, and everything that falls on the left side of the high point you say is idiosyncratic, so you discard that segment. But that part that doesn't follow the rules is where I always get hung up, because I'm interested in that other part as well! It doesn't disprove orthodox terminology, it just says that your proof isn't 100 percent and you had better be careful that you don't include every- body because doing so is an oversimplification. That's what stigma is all about. It's an assumption that anybody that has a particular label attached to them is going to act and respond in a particular way. Stigmas and stereo types are also what prejudice is—and what I'm saying about loneliness is that there really doesn't need to be that same kind of stigma, because it's a more universal condition.

I have been taking you with me on this potpourri of life stories and experiences in the hope that you will make your own judgments about the essence of loneliness. I hope, by seeing how other people have experienced these feelings, you will see loneliness more clearly in terms of your own life and then be willing to look at some alterna- tive ways of perceiving and managing loneliness when you meet it face to face.

Let's look at some other aspects of loneliness which might help us in this. Some people, such as Tim Adams who is thirty-nine and a teacher, are in touch with their loneliness but are not overly distracted by it. Tim copes with his loneliness by being comfortably able to use fami- liar things in his environment to feel connected with im- portant people as part of his life.

"... You see, I see loneliness as not just missing one or two people—just a general kind of psychic waste- land, so to speak, you know what I mean. When you're feeling, like I say, just really missing something. When you're feeling blah! The extent of it is, it affects your whole organism as opposed to me getting along fairly well one weekend, doing a lot of work, and enjoying the people I'm with, but all the time missing a particular person. To me that isn't drastic loneliness, because the missing of the particular person doesn't completely wreck my psyche, you know what I mean. I'm still able to go on functioning. . .

"When I talk about loneliness, I have to look at somebody who is really feeling that, even for ten minutes or five minutes or a minute, just totally pervades . . . an all-pervasive kind of sense of loss . . . I feel that constantly when I go away to conferences or whenever I travel, getting to that strange place. Just the whole relating once again to space. Like the cat throws down her scent. A place where I haven't had my own scent thrown down. I am still in a foreign place where the marks of my ego aren't there, that I haven't incorporated yet into myself and thus been able to incorporate myself into it at those foreign places, and so the environmental strangeness overwhelms me.

"It sort of happens a lot—like if you and I went to San Francisco, and we each got a hotel room in a strange hotel. We went in there and I got in my hotel room and I didn't recognize anything. I just took my suitcase and I put it on one of the beds and I just took my coat and I hung it up and I just took a couple of the books I was reading, papers that I had with me in my briefcase, and I spread the things out on the dresser. All right? I did just that, and went out to eat. Afterwards when I came back for some reason, I went into the wrong room. Well, those things of mine aren't there. That's not my space. The other place is my space and I feel differently when I'm in the other's place, because that's where I put down my droppings, so to speak, that's where I laid out my stuff . . .

"All I know is, space is very important. And it must be because I think loneliness is one of those powerful feelings, so it has to be connected into loneliness, and probably, you know, all these things being attempts to avoid loneliness. . . ."

★ ★ ★

Sometimes I have been deeply touched by some un-expected little experience which has opened for me some of my own feelings about loneliness—a face once seen in a crowd—a lost voice. Often it is connected with actions I have not taken or some incident which keenly makes me feel my own separateness.

Such an experience happened last summer, after I had visited on Galiano Island, British Columbia, an older cousin whom I had not seen in almost twenty years. After my visit I had flown to San Francisco for a day before heading back to Boston. I was still feeling happy about the lovely week I had spent with my cousin. I had corre-sponded with her for years and loved her very much but our time together had ended. I was back in San Francisco, a city with lots of good memories of the time I had worked as a deck officer for the Matson Navigational Steamship Company, sailing on their ships out through the Pacific Ocean. So here I was, alone in this beautiful city, ... but my heart was back on Galiano Island, and I was remember-ing how I had run through the forest each morning of my visit.

Absentmindedly I entered a crowded cable car and stood close to a woman, two jostled strangers pressed together by people, buttocks touching, holding tight-ly to the straps above us. And yet, she could not know, in this moment of intimacy, that I loped with panther grace down a forest trail, somewhere far away.

My heart leapt in my chest as my imagination walked the trail led gently through shadows edged in sunlight. I saw a fawn bound across my path and giant trees thrust toward blue sky. Running had always brought me close into the rich essence of my life and I felt it now, as my thoughts ran toward and not away, feeling the soft connectedness of heel thump, lift and float.

It seemed that I had run for hours, and yet I felt refreshed. Shadows deepened and the trail led off toward what I knew must be the sea. Somehow this was comforting, and yet strangely, I think I was about to speak to someone very far back and distant in my life, when the jarring cable car tossed my stranger-companion and me together again.

In that instant I felt her pelvis deep against my thigh. Suddenly, I was very lonely and unsure. When I looked at her, she seemed to be crying gently to herself....

D.P.

★ ★ ★

I wondered what memory road she was treading but I did not ask. Finally the cable car stopped and I got off. To share momentary feelings with strangers can bring insights. To share communion with new friends can bring real self-discovery.

One very special day Bob Walters walked into my life. "Hobbled" into my life might be a more accurate statement. Either way, I found him an amazingly honest and intriguing man. Bob is thirty-five and single and he was born with part of his lower body paralyzed so he has trouble walking. When I first approached him about doing some taped interviews for my project I explained this whole thing about "confidentiality" and that I wouldn't use his real name, etc. He was astounded that I wouldn't use his real name, and said to me, "Of course, use my name!" But to be consistent, I haven't. Now, Bob is no ordinary man and that has nothing to do with his being five feet tall and weighs just under 300 pounds. I'd like to introduce you to Bob because he has a mind that is ten feet tall, and hearing his story from his own lips can be helpful in beginning to understand how individuals become lonely and how other people deal with it. Bob's story is unique, but the truths in it are the same for all of us.

"... I've done some bad or wrong or mistaken things in my life, and I'm sorry, and I wish I hadn't done them, and I forgave myself for them, and I'm more than willing to ask other people to forgive me, and I feel that any decent citizen will, and I'll do what I can to make amends. I'm sincerely sorry. That's all I can do. I'm only human. I can't turn back the clock and make the past nonexistent. You can't rewrite history. I mean, it happened and I feel that if you don't forgive me, if you're angry at me because of something I've done, I can look at that too. Your anger is not likely to kill me, and won't destroy my life, and you can't expect the whole world to love you. In fact, if you manage to find just two or three people in your whole life to love you, then you're doing well. But that being the case, I suddenly discovered I have no secrets.

"It necessitated going through my whole life, layer by layer until I got to the very deepest and darkest, finest, most ultimate scene you can get to, which in my case, was the fact that I hated my mother to the point that I'm wishing I murdered her, and the experience was that that emotion of hatred for a short period of time, perhaps half an hour, was unused. My mother, at this time, was already dead, but had she been alive and in front of me, I think I could have chopped her to pieces with a machete and roasted and eaten her, and that's not the whole story. There was also a feeling of love for my mother. A feeling of compassion and understanding of her, but for all the sins of omission and commission she and I had committed in our life together, there was a tremendous charge of hatred and anger that I spent my entire life denying in her presence, and finally just . . . I mean, in a way, I knew it was there.

"One of the problems that she had was that she was very undemonstrative to the point of being almost catatonic at times. I mean, a block of marble. You couldn't tell what was going on inside of her. She wouldn't talk about it, and she wouldn't share it in any readable way. And you can only guess, well, if I were she and I were in that position, what would I do or be like?

"That's a very chancy and subjective way of getting at other people's feelings, and anyway, after that experience, you know, after having been through what I considered the bottom of myself, I sort of said, 'Well, I forgive her for being her.' I forgive me for being me, and between us, we sort of are an extraordinary pair of mother and son and not exceptional in any sort of way, and if anything, a little better because maybe our standards were a little higher than some . . . and maybe we, or at least I on my part, felt so strongly about the many things just because my standards were so high, and that was nothing to be ashamed of, but to be proud of.

"Hey, I like to meet high standards. It is not a sin. Not having any standards to meet is a sin. Having very low standards is not sinful, but shooting for the moon is another thing, and forgiving yourself for not making it strikes me as being the essence of getting along in life and recognizing your own humanness. Having recognized that, and having decided that I would live with the fact that I wasn't God and never would be, I had no secrets, and I'm able to ask forgiveness of other people. Most people willingly extend it. The few who don't, well, I can't help that. I'll do what I can to accept what usually happens. At first, you avoid each other and you never see them again, and so you can't even remember who it is you had the problem with.

"Loneliness is a subject that I have given a great deal of thought to because I have experienced my life as having been alone all of it. I used to say, and still occasinally do, that I was raised in an orphanage that happened to be run by my parents, because that was the feeling. My father was both a lonely workaholic and an alcoholic, and I'm sure the two were related in ways that I'm unaware of. But they often are together, and this case—he was kind of never there for one reason or another. He was just out of touch. I mean, for the largest part of the day, it was physical unavailability and for a portion of the day it was the fact that the Second Coming would be required to get a response from him. And my mother had this problem with being sort of withdrawn and an undemonstrative person. You never got a sense of what she was thinking or feeling.

"Were they alive today, they would be in their mid-sixties, probably—but she was a housewife, she never thought of it as a job. Living as a bachelor all my life, I can tell you that it is a job. I mean, if you try to hire somebody to do it, you finally discover what an expense it is. She did it quite a while. She was a competent housewife, but the emphasis was, as was true of so many parents of their generation, with custodial duties, to see that the kids had clean clothes. They got new shoes every year. They wore rubbers when it rained. When they sniffled, you called the doctor. That seemed to be the end of it. That was the limit of her responsibilities. Oh, and she quoted a few Golden Rules about what you were supposed to do in life, and that was about the end of it. Well, it struck me at least as being very cold and unemotional. Very lonely existence, and at a very early age, I became aware of this and made all the usual childish attempts with which you break through the barrier.

"Well, I'm one of six children and interestingly enough, all six had identical experiences with my parents. It was not unique to me. It wasn't that I had especial difficulty with them that the others didn't. It was not related to my age—I'm the third child—and it's not related to my handicap, because the other five are not in any way handicapped. It was just the way my parents were. Now the other five compensated—all of them—by enjoying society. I mean, they all developed extra-familial interests, anyway, out of the family relationships. They sought companionship, love, whatever one gets. They sought it outside the family. Well, for me, because of my disability, I couldn't do that.

"It was apparent from a very early age that I was very different from the rest of the people on earth and that in a way, it was kind of funny. My initial experience of it was not that I was different, but that I was on the lower end of the spectrum. I couldn't run as fast or jump as high, I was shorter than, but part of. But they didn't see it that way, see . . . and the other kids, year by year, became more apparent. As far as they were

concerned, there was a qualitative difference between us. It wasn't just that I was a little slower and they weren't, and the feeling I got was that I was being pushed out.

"So, loneliness is a subject I have been aware of and dealt with all my life, and I've experienced it basically as a lack. I don't see loneliness as . . . Loneliness isn't something you ARE in life—loneliness is something you didn't DO in life, because of other people. . .

"I have a feeling, I'll never know the truth of this, but I have a feeling that throughout my mother's life, she loved my father, but he didn't love her, and I think she managed to sustain that one-way relationship throughout her natural lifetime. It cost her a great deal, and through her, us, her children. But again, I can't prove that. It's a difficult thing to do, but I'm sure there are many people who do it."

Bob's life is very different from most of ours. He has managed his physical problems with considerable courage. You can see the energy and enthusiasm he finds in the less athletic but just as nimble world of ideas. His talent is communicating and he does it very well.

This makes me realize that when I review events that might have made me lonely in the past, it's most useful to do this when it leads to understanding myself well enough to do something about it, as Bob has done.

Some years ago I participated in an informal afternoon with a group of graduate students who were doing short practice interviews with each other. The plan was to test the correlation between a person's early "life story" as it unfolded in the interview and the way the group saw this person functioning now. The members of this group would act as advisors to the interviewee. Here's how the second half of one of the interviews went.

"Are you comfortable with the people who are sharing this interview?"

"Yes."

"I'm ready for some recollections. Now let me tell

you how we will use the word 'recollection.' A recollection is sort of a vague memory of something that happened before the age of six."

"Well, somewhere in there is a sense of loneliness, and I'm not sure where it comes from. I remember it was activated once by the house next door to us burning down one night. We all woke up and the house was just in flames, and we were afraid that our house would be next."

"How old were you?"

"Probably about five or six. And I remember thinking what if that had been my parents, you know, where would that leave me. I recall the little boy that lived there. They all got out safely. But I remember thinking about him."

"O.K. Now what kind of a feeling did you have?"

"It was a feeling of fear, of abandonment."

"But you told us before that you had that feeling once when you were younger."

"Yes, but I had it again. The feeling of waking up and not having a bed or anything around me. The other thing I remember is the feeling of stupidity, which is secondary I think."

"Can you give me a specific instance?"

"I have a vague memory of sitting in a classroom in a school and knowing that we were supposed to be completing something, and I couldn't do it; and waiting for the time to be up and knowing what the teacher would say when she came around and saw that I hadn't done it. I remember feeling that way from the earliest year that I was in school."

"How old were you when you first remembered?"

"I'm guessing, probably about six or seven. One thing I'm remembering too is that even as a kid I did an awful lot of wandering. I would go off by myself and my family would get very worried. I remember once going down in a culvert under the railroad tracks because I loved to sing, loved the reverberating sound that my voice made in the hollow, and I called and yelled. It was very melodious. It was dusk when my mother found me there. She was very angry."

"O.K. You said you remember when you came to live with your parents after being in the orphanage."

"I remember coming up the walk, up to this house, and I remember a certain kind of oval window on the front porch and somebody sitting in the frame of the window. It was recessed, and my mother somehow lifted me up and I was sitting there with her."

"How did you feel?"

"I was feeling scared, but it felt good to be there. When my adopted sister came two years later I was sitting in that same oval window. I remember my mother bringing her home."

"Do you remember having any reoccurring dreams when your sister came home?"

"No, but I used to have nightmares. A dream about a feeling that I had. It was something that had to do with my fingers, and there was a special way that I had to hold them. If I didn't hold them right, something would happen."

"What would happen?"

"I don't really remember, but it wasn't good."

"O.K. I think that's significant food for your own recollection of being in a classroom and the teacher saying to do something and you couldn't do it, and you had a feeling of not being able to do it. You felt stupid and incompetent. If you don't hold your hands just right there are expected to be bad times. And what was the other topic?"

"The other was a dream of being chased around a bunch of cabins. Running slow motion and having to lean way forward into the wind in order to get anywhere. I don't remember who was chasing me. I had that dream many, many times and it was always the same dream. I got lost somehow. It was always around some buildings that were always square."

"What else?"

"I remember there were times when if I pumped my arms hard enough, I could fly and get away. I remember this reoccurring feeling that at times I could fly if I really tried hard enough. I could really soar."

(Interviewer now speaks to the group.)

"I see that as part of Dick's lifestyle that he may feel he can do anything he wants if he just keeps at it and works hard enough."

"One of the ethics of the family, which I had forgotten, was that we could do anything if we worked at it. It took diligence."

"You were talking earlier about the problem of reading, and your dyslexia. How did you overcome that problem?"

"I remember having a special tutor. When I was at home in bed recuperating. Can you believe this, she had me weaving baskets as well. I was ashamed to be doing that. And my family was so worried about me that they took me from Scranton to the Massachusetts General Hospital in Boston to a Child Psychiatric Unit. The irony of course, is that as an adult I did some training as a therapist in the Adult Psychiatric Unit of that same hospital. I never got over the irony of that situation.

"But as a kid, I thought I must be pretty bad if they have to bring me to this place. It sure helped me to emphathize with people who felt bad about themselves."

"You felt that you were a pretty bad person to be brought to Mass. General?"

"Not so much that I was bad, but that I must be pretty stupid and screwed up because of my not being able to read or do many of those scholastic things the other kids could do at that age. It was kind of lonely, feeling so outside."

"Then can you remember thinking how you felt after you began to be able to read better?"

"I didn't begin to learn to read until I was sent out to the Out-of-Door School. Then I began to read—and I read and read and nobody could stop me. It was then that the full world just really came into view. I was excited. But the whole possibility of education just opened up to me in Florida. I had a tremendous desire to learn and that it was fun. And I think I didn't feel so lonely then."

"Life is a big adventure."

"Very much. Like wanting to be a sailor. This was one thing I always wanted to be as a kid. I used to lie up in the fields on this farm in Pennsylvania and just dream of going to the Naval Academy at Annapolis. Although I was afraid I couldn't get into Annapolis, I filled notebooks full of nautical nomenclature."

"Would you like to help do some summary here with the help from the group? How you view your world and all of that?"

"Yes."

"I'll start. I think Dick likes to be accepted by people and feels comfortable with 'family.' You have a good feeling among your relatives, and it's very important for them to like you."

"I think that's true."

"You have some legitimate fears for feeling the fear of abandonment because something has happened that you do not remember when you were very young. The problem of having a reading difficulty at an early age is also probably something that you are still working through—not the problem, the feeling."

"Yes, that's true."

"I keep thinking how this relates very much to this whole issue of the vagabond sailor part of it, when you got a sense of being on some kind of voyage which you aren't sure how it quite began—and searching, a lot of searching. You said you still are curious about what your natural mother was like. You never did find her?"

"No. But I'm not so curious anymore. I've thought about it numerous times, but I don't really need to know anymore."

"I'd like you to make a mental picture, and in it you are sailing. You are out there alone on the water."

"I've come to appreciate a lot of things. It's peaceful and I know what I'm about; kind of like coming from darkness into light."

"I think the early recollection of when you were in the culvert may have significance to your being on land because you say you were lonely at times, and yet, when you were there by yourself, alone on a

sailing ship, you know that you are in control of what's going on. I think, for you, that's the important difference between being alone and being lonely, and being alone and feeling good. *The issue in terms of loneliness is still having some feeling of control.*"
(Speaking to the group)

"Do you think this short interview worked? Do you know Dick any better than you did? Do you want to add anything?"
(One of the men answered)

"Yes, there is a part of Dick like I have a part of me, that likes to play the free-spirit child, and I find that beautiful in Dick. He has a great sense of having fun. For no particular purpose, just to have fun. He enjoys that, and I do, too. Without any work at the other end or some great purpose."

"Are you comfortable with all we've done? This is a non-threatening kind of way of getting some understanding about what's going on with people. It may also offer them the opportunity to change things that they are not satisfied with in their present life. In doing this you are only viewing the world of one person. One view of Dick's life, for example, is one of losses and of searching. You see that Dick's view of life is an adventure; and that's that. He puts his history to use, as we all can.

SIX

PEOPLE OF THE MIRROR

9:00 a.m.
There is a whiplash sting in the clear November air.
I am going through my morning mail.
Inadvertently, I open her letter first —

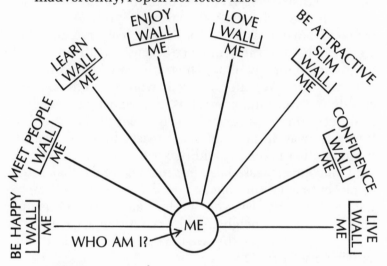

*"I built the walls.
I'm afraid.
I don't know how to climb them!!!
Dick, who am I?
I'm like a mirror,
I feed on other people's
feelings about me to live.
I see other people
as a mirror of myself.
The hurt, fear, pain, anger,
is all that's mine.
How do I begin my life?"*

Marleen

"God," I thought, "Marleen, how can I ever answer your questions? You can't rebuild someone. You cannot change what has happened to them. *All of us have to begin where we are right now*, and with whatever we have within us to work with." It is hard to convince someone that life is always at the end of the tunnel.

I knew, however, that answering her questions as best as I could was exactly what I had to do. I held her letter in my hand for a long while before beginning to put words to my feelings:

Do you remember when I told you that bit about my own voyage of discovery? Well, one of the beautiful things that I've been able to discover, and I think it is true for you, too, is that we are *not* searching for who we really are, and if we are, it's a sham and an avoidance because such a quest can't be answered for any of us. The truth is we knew all along who we were. We didn't accept who we were, and we couldn't or wouldn't admit this. So, we denied ourselves the nicest things we ever had, the *real* us, and tried to throw it away in favor of some masked-marvel face we thought other people would like better than our real one. And, of course, masks keep us separated rather than bring us closer to what we want and need. How close can you be with a shield between you and love and companionship? Our loneliness is heightened by the distance barrier and knowing deep inside that we have labeled ourselves "unsatisfactory," not "O.K."

What we really desire is to connect with others honestly—to allow our authentic selves out from behind those terrible masks. This is a bedrock issue, because I've too often seen people who are (or would be) accepted by other people but are not accepted by themselves, and they remain miserable and lonely.

Loneliness only terrifies because it says something about us. This is not something we need to continue to hide from, however. You hear people saying, "I need to find out who I am," or "I'm trying to find myself." Any kid in the street could have told them who they were. The clash comes when we are carrying around in our heads the picture of the perfect person we think we should be, and the reality is the person we see in the mirror.

Accept Yourself

We're not dealing with ignorance here, we're dealing with concealment. I think of loneliness in terms of a statement made by Pogo in the comic strips: "We have met the enemy and he is us." The majority of people are more willing to forgive others for not being everything they wanted than they are willing to forgive themselves. Gentleness with our self is what we need.

People don't make changes easily, and often not until their present situation becomes intolerable. Yet, it is so incredibly self-defeating and energy-wasting to stay wallowed in misery. As I see it, fear is one of the things that increases our sense of alienation. We feel we're without resources. Pain is to the body what fear is to the mind. Pain tells us something is wrong. Fear tells us there may be something wrong; change may be necessay, either in us or in our environment. They are both signals, but the trouble is that we tend to distort, or misinterpret them because we are lonely and loneliness hurts, and we're sure that tomorrow has to be filled with even more pain.

At a deeper level, we generally know why we're lonely. We are afraid, not so much of the loneliness, but of the cause of our loneliness. So, perhaps, we never get to the first step in dealing with it: *The first step is admitting the problem to ourselves, and attempting to define its origins more clearly.* It is hard, of course, to ask ourselves "What is it that *I* am doing (or not doing) now that keeps me stuck in this lonely state?"

When lonely people look into their mirror, they often do not see what they want to see. What they want to see is a heroic, happy individual. Yet they see misery. One part of them says, "I want to be independent and self-sustaining," and another says, "I have this terrible need and I want help."

When you look closely, there really are very few, if any, of the "Rock of Gibraltar" types around. In many ways, the so-called integrated person doesn't exist, because the integrated person is not always consistent. You accept the contradiction when you are integrated because you accept what you know yourself to be, functioning well but full of contradictions. You accept the whole ball of wax and it is acceptance that holds it all together.

I am stressing *acceptance* of our natural inconsistency because it relates to our beginning to manage lonely feelings. What is the opposite of acceptance? It's rejection, and that's what I see loneliness is often all about. It is when you and I reject ourselves, and other people may reject us, too. But here's the real issue—It's when *we* move away from *them* that we close ourselves out, especially if somewhere deep inside we really want to be closer to them. There are myriad reasons why anybody might reject anything, but they all come under the rubric of loneliness, if they lead to rejection of ourselves.

When you can accept yourself first, and then accept other people, it becomes much easier for them to feel accepting of you. You see, you *cannot* change someone else, no matter how much you try. *You can change only yourself,* and by doing so, improve the climate between you and that other person to the point where they may feel reinforced enough to make changes in themselves.

I know that the pain I've had in my life seemed very real and deep at the time. Sometimes I hit it and often I felt self-defeated. But I think now, in looking back, that such moments of anguish were the most valuable things that ever happened to me.

What comes to mind is that lonely year I spent in the hospital and later recuperating from a broken back. Already at age ten, two years behind in school, feeling stupid because I couldn't read at all well at the time. I saw my friends going on about their own lives and seeming to leave me behind.

Surviving experiences such as these gave me what I

would like to believe is a depth that I otherwise would not have had, and I think now that I am the richer for it. It has come not out of placid acceptance, but of my saying, "Here you are now, with this good stuff and this bad stuff, and I accept that in you. I'm saying to you, *let's use what you have now and move on."*

A friend said to me once:

> "I'll tell you something that kept me going throughout my life. It's the feeling that if it could hurt as much as it did, think what happiness can be like."

And, you know, the constructive and collective power of hope is in there too. Hope is a part of faith.

Marleen, Harold, Barbara, "The Woman Who Sits Alone," and the others you have been reading about are *People of the Mirror.* They exist. They each do what they can to survive and feel good. They are, in truth, like most of us.

The analogy of the mirror illuminates a common experience and highlights why we make loneliness so hard to deal with. We often see it and ourselves through a curious haze. It isn't that the mirror image is imperfect. It is rather that we often alienate ourselves from that image, wishing that it were better than it was, fearful that it only looks better and really isn't. Or we fear that our lonely feelings will diminish us in terms of the image we present. What we see, mirrored as our authentic selves is unacceptable; so we go about trying desperately to make the person we see in that glass into what we think other people want to see, . . . glass into what we think other people want to see, . . .

You might say that our susceptibility to loneliness is in direct proportion to our inability to accept the person we see in the mirror.

SEVEN

THE ANATOMY OF
LONELINESS

"Master, how is it that you see so clearly?"
"I close my eyes."
(Words from a Dean Shapiro Cartoon)

"Professor, how is it that you see things so clearly?"
"I open my eyes and monitor the data."
(Words from a Dean Shapiro Cartoon)

I would like to report a dream. In the dream I am only ten years old, but I feel much older. I have come downstairs this particular Sunday morning with one aim in mind. I have decided the only hope for me is to take a fresh look at the stale ready-made answers to the perplexing questions I have about life. My parents and my sister are sitting at the breakfast table. I see that my box of Raisin Bran is at its usual place by my plate. My mother's look is one of patience—I'm thinking, she already knows the kind of questions I will ask her, so I plunge right in, believing I'm entitled to answers.

"I heard the telephone ring a lot last night," I said. "Will people always call us. Will they walk along the sidewalk in front of our house? Will there always be mail for us in our mailbox?" The words poured out and I couldn't seem to stop. "Why is it that the Lone Ranger never really rides alone? What did God answer when Jesus cried out those last words from the Cross?"

95

Suddenly I began to feel confused, and I saw my sister staring at me as though she too had been waiting to ask those very same questions. In an instant the scene changed—you know how dreams are—I was singing a song softly while my mother reached out to touch my shoulder. "I am a rock," I sang. "I am an island." I stopped and looked over at my dad and I was saying, "Why do words go like that? A rock feels no pain? An island never cries?"

"You were born a hundred years old," my father said, and then he added, "We're always protecting ourselves from something, aren't we? Do you remember when we used to talk about the dark at the top of the stairs and you were afraid to go up alone until we explained that things often seem very dark when we don't understand? He glanced over at my mom for a second and then continued, "We used to tell you that you will always feel us in your presence even when we can't actually be there." The dream went on and at the end it seemed as though my mother finally answered all of my questions, but I'm not sure how. I do remember her saying quite clearly to me, "You have been talking about loneliness, haven't you?"

★ ★ ★

There are subtle characteristics of the experience of loneliness that begin with a paradox such as my dream-memory—the effects of loneliness are observable when loneliness itself is not. Unlike the symptoms we see in depression where there are often observable barometers such as a lowered pulse rate, heart rate, basic metabolic rate, pupil dilation, loss of appetite, loss of weight etc., loneliness describes a feeling state that isn't so outwardly observable. Quite often the feeling doesn't seem to come from any real response to the external environment, it's there and it becomes a point of awareness that frequently initiates new sensitivities within us. I believe that loneliness is a feeling state that everyone has experienced at some level. Loneliness naturally can be a pure reaction to some real event in our lives. Since we cannot observe loneliness itself, we usually speak of the product of loneliness. Questioning our popularity, for example might be one outcome of our sense of loneliness. We all need people and when we don't have them, we're alone and possibly lonely. In my experience, however, there are a few people who feel relief when they are alone. For them it is often their defense against relationships which require closeness or intimacy, and since they are afraid of this, they tend to seek isolation. Perhaps in this particular circumstance they do not experience the loneliness as such, but they are the exception, not the rule, for they have cut themselves off from feeling-level relationships in the mistaken belief that they will lead only to pain. The ability to give or receive love is closely tied up with one's sense of confidence that one will not be rejected or seen as acceptable if one reaches out and expresses caring feelings to someone else. There are qualities to loneliness and feeling lonely which we need to try to understand.

There were times when I asked myself if the feeling of loneliness was the result of an entirely appropriate loss, such as when my adoptive father and mother died. The result of this particular lonely feeling came out of a real and normal life crisis. It wasn't going to be a problem forever to me and I knew that I was accepting it in such a way that it would not continue as a crippling force in my life. The boundaries of this type of pain and the knowledge of its source have an acceptable reality with which we all can deal.

We all have an idea in our minds of what is acceptable as well as what is "normal." This is one of the judgments we make that protects our feelings, since it helps us define what behavior is not appropriate to get into, and what feelings jar with our sense of well-being. In order to feel totally free, we have to know what our own boundary system is as well as that of others. We also need to know that people will react in relatively reliable patterns so that we don't have to worry.

There is another more persistent quality of loneliness not so directly related to some recent loss, as in my first example. All loneliness comes out of some sense of unwanted loss, real or imagined, and this second, more pervasive loneliness often develops from a long-time sense of deprivation. We may, for example, be overly sensitive to early childhood, adolescent or adult experiences of personal failures and/or our lack of closeness to important people. We all share in varying degrees, good or bad feelings about our past. Sometimes it is hard to resolve the bad feelings and this may leave us somewhat confused, believing ourselves to be inadequate, and fearful as to how things will work out. These factors, then, have a relationship to how we experience loneliness, in that the more we are able to work through these negative feelings about ourselves and our history, the easier it becomes to accept the inevitable set-backs or transient periods of loneliness that we all must face.

In between the extremes of degree in loneliness as a simple irritation that we can live with on the one hand, and the frightening, all-consuming loneliness and void from which we can see no escape on the other, is a middle ground. Here a broken love affair, being fired from a job, the loss of a friendship, some personal rejection, separation by death, distance, or one's own guilt, from other important people, etc., may leave us feeling very much alone and doubting our capacity to bear it—but bear it we do and many times we go on successfully.

A friend of mine describes her own experiences with this more moderate feeling of loneliness brought about by a special crisis in her family: "I can't honestly remember the feeling of the terrible loneliness that people talk about. I don't know why. Why can't I remember that? I guess it is because I have never really been alone, in any real sense. Isn't that funny. I never thought about it, to tell you the truth, but when Rodger was sick and in the hospital was probably the loneliest time of my life. Isn't that funny that I didn't even think about that. There were five months that I was alone. But I wasn't, really. The kids were there. My friends would call me and say, "Come to our house. Come visit," or "Let's go out. Let's do something." I didn't want that, and I didn't want to feel guilty about it either, but I did! I was tired. Exhausted from everything that I was doing, and what I really wanted was to have somebody come over and be with me, so I wouldn't be alone after the kids went to bed. I was thinking about that the other day— I've gone through a lot of different emotions, and especially the loneliness while Rodger was hospitalized. There was a lot of loneliness after he came back, too, because he wasn't the same, and adjusting to this new person, who was not the person that I knew before, was difficult. But that seems to be behind me now."

The issue of guilt in connection with loneliness is an important topic in itself. Essentially, it takes a reasonably high level of character development, I think, to struggle with feelings of guilt and not have remorse affect one's action. Perhaps it is the price we pay for caring about ourselves and others, and wanting to live honestly. Like loneliness, guilt is loaded with useful messages. So, if your guilty feelings affect the way that loneliness is for you, there is some comfort in realizing that you have the ability (yes, I see it as an asset), and conscience to know what is or is not good for you, and to base this judgment, not just in terms of yourself, but in relation to the people you affect. This is often quite a different experience from the "empty" kind of loneliness described by people with more narcissistic, that is, overly-invested-in-themselves kinds of personalities, who simply are not so much aware of guilt issues as you might be. In either case, however, new sensitivities can be developed when we are willing to stop and look at how we operate in the real world.

Where on this Loneliness Continuum you find yourself now will largely depend on how you interpret lonely feelings and how you feel about yourself. I have found that there is a correlation between loneliness and the degree to which we feel depressed, shy, self-conscious, anxious and self-devaluing. The greater the susceptibility to loneliness, the more prominent one or more of these negative attributes appear to be.

This makes me remember a fascinating interview I did recently with Arleen Framie, a thirty-eight-year-old, single woman I met at an educational training program. We seemed to hit it off immediately and later that same evening, we taped this interview. I had sensed that Arleen was troubled by something but I didn't know what at first. This small section of our interview will give you a perspective of one of the issues with which she was dealing.

"I was only ten when we went into the hospital. They rolled my father out in a wheelchair and when he came in, he was crying, but the cry he had was a sick cry. It was a strange sound, and it really rattled me. I was with my mother, and as they rode him in closer and settled him in the chair, she said to me, 'He wants to hold you.' Now I knew that was my father and I wanted to be close to him, but I became petrified at that point because I also wanted to leave the room, and as I went out, he began that cry, and all I could think of was that he's in that wheelchair. I had a fear of hurting him by going to him, and sitting hard on him, and this is what I felt. But I kept hearing my mother saying, 'Go, he wants to hold you.'

"That one experience is what left me with the biggest pain that I ever had as far as loneliness goes. I really believe that it was the one moment of my life that created the feeling for me that I was incapable of loving or being loved, because I failed to go to him and I had nothing to give him. I would say that this is probably part of my guilt after my mother died, why I had no purpose in life, because my greatest desire was to die.

"Being Christian is what kept me alive, the fact that you can't take your own life, the fact that I loved God more than anything else, but yet to live was death as far as I was concerned. It was a matter of living to wait for the moment of death. That's what loneliness was

for me; no people really there, no one to really communicate with.

"When you're lonely, there is no sense of whole-
ness in you. I guess there is just a gaping need. It hurts
even if there is silence. It's a strange thing, it's like, all
you can really tell about loneliness is the tremendous
feelings it leaves you and, am I afraid? Maybe that's
why I went into a lot of confusion. I'd never really
dealt with it—no one had ever come up to me to ask
me how he could help. Lonely people have to become
beggars, more or less."

For almost thirty years, Arleen carried feelings of guilt
over not being able to respond to her father. On several
occasions she came very close to taking her own life. In
many ways, she had become a loner, afraid to trust becoming involved in a male-female relationship. She is only just
beginning to put the pieces of her fear together in a form
that she can understand.

There is a wide gap between her desired perception of
herself as lovable and loving and her actual withdrawal
from her father, which she perceived as demonstrating her
own unlovableness and inability to give love back. Arleen's loneliness and depression immobilized her, she was
mired deep in her own misery and was sure that there was
no way that things might change for her. To have suggested to her at that time that what she needed was only to
"get out and get moving, find some friends to be with,"
would, I feel, have been doomed to failure.

Imagining the Possibility of Change

Again, the question, how to start? We have to begin at
the beginning, I think, and for Arleen this was an attempt
to modify her behavior in some new way—making an
attempt to first create a vision of the *possibility of change*.
This is almost the hardest thing she will ever have to do to
manage loneliness. To keep working the old tapes of
failure and badness over and over in her head only keeps
old wounds from healing.

People often surprise themselves as they are talking with me about their loneliness feelings. Quite often they discover that *their problem isn't with loneliness itself, so much as it is that they are demoralized.* These people gradually come to realize that their discomfort isn't coming from somewhere outside of them, from some other person, for example, but begins inside of them. Perhaps in some way they know a part of this already, but in order to feel in control of things, they rationalize their feelings, blaming some other person or thing. I wouldn't say this was the usual case, but I think each of us has seen people who have trouble owning up to their part in things.

I like the analogy of relating our thinking process to a radar scanner which is continually scanning everything that happens around us. We label all of the various data coming into our brain's perceptions. Naturally, we hope to continue receiving good input, but when we are not, our system lets us know that something is wrong, corrections are in order.

Suppose, for example, you are a housewife, alone at home right now. Frankly, you've observed that your relationship with your husband hasn't been close enough for some time now and you've been wondering why. There is a kind of hunger in you to not feel so separate and yet things seem out of your control. You consciously or unconsciously are feeling left out and worried about this, and this process of worry becomes experienced as the particular inner stress or anxiety that is loneliness. Many people describe it as an awareness of a "blank space" inside of them. Something needed is missing. There is a personal emptiness and feeling of distance that I characterize as the *depressive lacunae* of loneliness. (In using the word "depression" here, I am referring, in particular, to one major feature, which is a feeling of sadness.) Within the person feeling loneliness there is a sense of unwanted aloneness, personal diminishment, sadness and pain— reason enough to call loneliness a *problem state.*

At its most observable extreme, one of the major underlying characteristics of such a state of loneliness is a feeling of acute or chronic anxiety which stems from unresolved depression over an imagined or real loss. This loss threatens our sense of identity and opens to us the specter of our helplessness in fulfilling our primary need to be part of some meaningful relationship. The hyper activity we often see in lonely people is a way of warding off that anxiety.

This experience of loneliness is always at odds with some part of our normal needs to feel: in control of our lives, close to one special person, accepted in some network of friends, and appreciated for what we are doing. Each of us needs to feel that our deeds have meaning and value that can both energize and validate us, and that we can look forward to pleasure or to fun. We know that we are lonely when the lack of one of these qualities brings us to the point where we recognize, "I'm lonely." If we are not aware of lost areas of relatedness we are not experiencing loneliness per se, but if we are feeling uneasy or are in some emotional pain, it could well be a clue to something that is a precondition to loneliness, or something akin to loneliness, such as depression or grief.

Either of these last two emotional states can be brought on by many of the same kinds of issues that trigger loneliness, and in fact, the more extreme our feelings of loneliness become, the more we become depressed. This seems especially true of the sadness aspect, or when depressed people turn their anger about losses or failures back against themselves and in doing so, begin self-deprecating cycles. We are on the fine edge here however, because I do believe that, quite naturally, there is a point in which we are often feeling very balanced and good about ourselves, and yet, are still aware of the loneliness factor in our lives, but are not morbid about it. At times we are simply conscious of the reality of loneliness and its force upon us but are not agonized by it. It is the matter of the degree to which loneliness controls us that can cause feelings of ennui and helplessness.

I would like to point out that I view the *loneliness* state as related to *depression* in that it includes at some level, a degree of dejection and pain, and yet it is less acute than the conception of depression because, in loneliness, there is much less tendency to become emotionally or physically incapacitated and unable to interact at all with other people. The withdrawal from reality that you see in acute depression is a kind of "last ditch" attempt to ward off any further painful loss. Often just the reverse is true in loneliness, the lonely individual tries desperately to deal with the situation by trying to stay in circulation, perform his or her duties, and expends considerable energy attempting to keep life on an even keel.

The discomfort of loneliness may sometimes be felt as a physical tension, inability to stay quiet, stomach pain, "sour lemon" taste, feeling of emptiness, headache, etc. This is the body's way of responding to the discomfort of a painful emotional state. More graphic reactions due to worry can be found in other common psychosomatic reactions such as the "diarrhea of fear" or the "constipation of anger."

Feeling that things are out of control is a common feature in loneliness. Perhaps finding oneself alone when solitude isn't satisfying. At times, I've noticed this myself when there is no one in the house but me. I'll sense a disquieting feeling that I can't quite put my finger on, and yet, I feel a sort of slight physical restlessness and emotional hollow which seems to lead me unconsciously to act by finding a substitute for physical comfort and perhaps raiding our refrigerator. Sometimes I'm not even hungry, but I become aware that I wish someone were around. Food has long been associated as a "filling in" substitute when something is missing and we are feeling empty and lonely. I have a strong feeling that anyone who is overweight to a large (no pun intended) degree, with the exception of a very few people with certain thyroid or other physiological problems, has a loneliness problem of considerable impact which isn't satisfied but is compensated for through overeating.

The depressed person's energy is invested very much in her- or himself. The person's desires move inward and he she is more apt to be involved in self-rumination than is the lonely person. If, however, the anguish of loneliness becomes extreme enough, features of depression become more and more prominent. This is not to say that the lonely individual's energy is not also self-directed because it is; however, when we are lonely we are more likely to seek something we feel to be missing, or to attempt to find or satisfy this need. The thrust of the lonely person's actions is usually towards goal-directed solutions, whereas the depressed person may act distractedly without direction or hope. In both cases, however, these varying activities are still designed to ward off anxiety. The depressed person often shows less of a repertory of behavior patterns and hangs on to these few rigidly. Although I have seen and treated lonely people who did not appear depressed, I have never seen or treated a depressed person who did not feel some sense of isolation.

There is a pertinent question to be looked at here. Is loneliness a cause of problems or a symptom of problems? I think we have two answers to the question, neither of which is clear-cut or mutually exclusive.

People who seem to demonstrate fragility and insecurity in their character and behavior appear to arrive at the point of loneliness as a symptom of problems that are often discernible to others, if not to themselves. The experience of loneliness as a terrible emptiness or void seems most often to occur in people who are in that borderline state where their sense of personal identity is clouded, and they have obvious trouble coping and dealing with reality. The central experience here is one of vulnerability, even rage perhaps, at feeling so empty and unable to manage the buffetings that life brings. There is no sense of the good self or proper action to relieve pain. It is my belief that nobody gets to this extreme state without first being aware of a strong sense of rejection, differentness, or loneliness.

At the other end of the scale are those people for whom loneliness often appears to be the cause of their problems. They seem generally to be more stable, clear-headed, and with a greater capacity to make significant attachments to other people. Such individuals appear more truly caring, unselfish and involved in the welfare of those with whom they associate. They are less egocentric. Nonetheless, though they manage their lives quite normally, they too become subject to some situations of loss and vulnerability as does everyone else. How they respond will depend upon their coping mechanisms.

It is often difficult to separate feelings of *loneliness* from *grief*, and in fact, feelings of loneliness are related to and accompany the very normal and necessary mourning process that we all go through after some major loss. In grief, as in loneliness, it is important that we understand the need to deal with our feelings of pain. The initial step in beginning to manage any loss is first to recognize its reality. When we mourn for what we have lost, we are accepting what we once had or wanted, acknowledging that it was important for us, and that now we are sadly left with only the feelings and memory of its existence.

Of course, we never completely stop missing important things which are now gone. We can only learn to accept and go on. Suppose, for example, you hold a "Dear John" letter in your hands right now. In mourning our losses, we generally go through stages which we can identify as parts of an orderly process of working through these feelings—nature's way of healing. The process of grief has several stages. First, disbelief—then perhaps the need to deny that the loss took place. Quite normally after this stage we may experience feelings of anger and guilt over the loss that we have suffered and over our imagined part in this. Nostalgia and regret may follow, in which the lost object becomes over-idealized, making our loss appear even greater. We ponder how things might have been if we had been different; we reminisce about how they were; we may feel anger at the departed for abandoning us, and gradually, if our denial is not too strong, we re-shape our perception of what was lost into a rememberance that we can accept as real. There is a necessary progression to the grieving process and if we do not allow ourselves to move through it we should take great care to find out why.

Grief work needs to be accomplished in spite of the cultural emphasis placed on inhibiting normal expressions of sadness. I, for one, think our cultural values have also affected our honest experience of loneliness in that they encourge a dishonest kind of outward stoicism which is unnatural and damaging. I remember surprising someone once when I was asked what my criteria of manliness was and I answered by saying, "Above all else, the ability to be honest and not to have to hide feelings."

It is not unnatural to expect that the person who feels lonely and forsaken will temporarily lose some degree of personal self-esteem—because a person important to our life has left us, perhaps we feel responsible or diminished by the separation, and now there is a void where there wasn't one before. We can regain our self-esteem as we learn to accept this loss and go on. The medium through which this reorganization of our feelings takes place is always in the context of other relationships and a large part of our recovery is belief that we can find something or someone else meaningful.

Hopefully, in exploring the anatomy of loneliness, we can come to a point where we can say, "O.K., yes, I may very well feel lonely now. I don't like it, but I know something about loneliness that I didn't know before—and part of what I recognize is that, bad as I feel right now, I don't need to be intimidated by it, tricked by it—I'm putting it to use instead of being used by it."

You could say that *at the heart of loneliness is a sense of void and separation, and that anxiety over these is the basic problem*, because no one wants to face the threat of unchosen isolation or loss. I do not view loneliness as a pathological condition, although I recognize that we can worry ourselves "sick" in the sense that in our anxiety we may lose perspective of what is real and what is not. To me, loneliness is not a "clinical" term, it is an effective feeling state, part of which involves anxiety.

Anxiety usually starts with some problem in our social environment which we begin to perceive as somehow threatening. Almost invariably it is a result of having incomplete data from which to make a satisfactory assessment. When our sense of reality is blurry, it leaves us uncertain and vulnerable to the tendency to misinterpret events. It's like a balloon that gets filled with too much hot air and then, BANG! Feelings of loneliness are full of this kind of endless, futile speculation about all the possible reasons why our perceptions of what is happening aren't jibing with what we expected or wanted. The anxiety of loneliness is often built on just such filaments of self-doubt and distortion.

We create our own worry system through all the mental images we dream up to try to explain what is happening. This energy we expend in unreasonable worry is energy that must be stolen from the production of other possibly more satisfying things we might choose to do. One of the insidious things about most forms of worry and self-doubt is how incredibly self-defeating it can become if we let it.

As we focus in on our own negative characteristics, we tend to trust ourselves less. Then it becomes harder to reach out with the confidence that people will like us and believe us to be normal. We feel more and more separate and alone. Around us inanimate objects such as clocks or other things may seem to be going all wrong. It is at times like these that we are apt to try to medicate our bad feelings away instead of working through them to find out why we have such feelings in the first place. There are all kinds of escapist medications; one that is often lethal to our system is alcohol, as any member of Alcoholics Anonymous can attest. This is not to underestimate the similar addictive problems of hard drug users, or the equally serious problem of the over-abuse of prescription and over-the-counter drugs, which have become a way of life for many lonely and depressed persons in our country—contra-productive, short-time substitutes for long-term solutions to things which seem painfully missing.

Forms of Loneliness

I do not find that there are really two or three specific kinds of loneliness which are each different from the other in any clearly distinctive form. Many names have been used in attempting to differentiate separate types of loneliness, and I will give you some samples of these. These names do not actually describe loneliness itself, but rather the general experience in which such distressing feelings are presumed to have originated. Popularly described as:

The loneliness of *"Emotional Isolation"*—pain caused by the absence of a specific cherished person. (The only "cure" seeming to be the return or replacement of the lost person.)

The loneliness of *"Social Isolation"*—pain caused by severance from some form of social group. (Again "cured" by re-establishment with the lost group or some new replacement group.)

"Existential Loneliness"—existential awareness of the human condition that we are born alone and must die alone.

"Primary Hunger Loneliness"—psychoanalytically viewed despair and loneliness over the lost comfort of our mother's womb.

The list goes on—

Terri Schultz, in her book, *Bitter Sweet*, describes a useful guideline that Professor William Sadler, Jr., offered her in regard to origins of loneliness:

Social —	when you are excluded from a group.
Cultural —	when you feel cut off from a tradition, from familiar values and roots (the loneliness of immigrants and travelers);

Cosmic —   when you feel the universe is absurd, life is
                  pointless, God is lost (the loneliness of the
                  existentialist); and

Psychological — when you feel alienated from yourself and out
                  of touch with your true nature.

We might also attempt to differentiate loneliness into
degrees of severity and frequency with names such as:

"Chronic Loneliness"—a long-time pattern that per-
sists. (Usually thought to originate because of early
childhood development problems. As a result of these
deficiencies in upbringing, the individual is now felt
to be hampered by having less mature personality and
therefore has less capacity to cope with problems.)

"Pathologic Loneliness"—as with "chronic loneliness," this description is a long-time favorite of clini-
cians who intend to emphasize the duration and ongoing morbidity which surrounds this depressive
"illness." The description implies the under-deve-
loped character and "pathology" of this lonely individual.

"Transient Loneliness"—a periodic or short-term pattern. (Generally viewed as less severe and much more
"normal" than "chronic loneliness.")

"Authentic Loneliness" —the reasonable and normal
loneliness that most people experience over their lifetime. Usually considered similar to the transient and
passing feelings which come about through reasonable losses.

All of these various terms are value judgments which try
to get at the polarities in loneliness which seem most
observable. Both "transient" and "authentic" loneliness,
for example, are assumed generally to be experienced with
a lesser degree of severity and frequency than the other two
classifications. Also, they fit more easily into what has
been called the *Situational Theory of Loneliness*, in which
it is presumed that regardless of personality, intelligence,

life experiences, etc., we are all liable to suffer from loneliness when painful situations arise.

On the other hand, we have what has been referred to as the *Characterological Theory of Loneliness*, into which "Chronic" and "Pathological" loneliness would be placed, since people classified this way are more likely to be viewed as "loneliness prone," because of personality deficiencies.

In spite of the damaging labels and implications that these definitions imply, it is my belief that self-defeating patterns of behavior can be overcome, and that no one needs to make a life long vocation out of loneliness.

We can take heart from this consoling observation which has been attributed to author/psychiatrist, Freida-Fromm Reichmann: "Even the 'sickest' people are not so different from their doctors—and there lives a neurotic child in the healthiest of us all."

Most everyone who has trained in psychiatry knows this very well, and in fact, has probably visualized with discomfort, transient signs of his own "pathology." This is especially horrifying during early training and is known as "first-year-itis." One of my contemporaries loves to remind me: "You know, Dick, I really thought I was reasonably normal until I got into this psychology business!"

It's the Interpretation That Counts

I believe that for our purposes here there is only the experience of loneliness which ranges from slight to extreme. Its experienced quality, depth and resultant effect upon us is not determined by a specific event so much as it is by the distinctive, philosophical/psychological make-up of our own personalities, our life experiences, and our ability to sort things out for ourselves. Neither does the acuteness of a particular lonely experience dictate a person's ability to handle it. How, for example, at times can a person manage grief and loneliness quite reasonably after we have lost someone we have loved very much. On the other hand, we may handle very badly, and with an extreme sense of pain and rejection, being fired from a job we have held only five months. The presumed originating experience, then, is not the major factor here so much as how we interpret the meaning of our loss and the way we handle it.

In searching for a key to the management of loneliness, I have, over the years, tried to look for patterns in the attitude and feelings that lonely people were sharing with me. I had hoped to develop some simple guidelines by which people could assess their feelings and then, on the basis of this, determine how to deal with what they had discovered. As I observed different peoples' behaviors and listened to their stories, common threads began to emerge—what had at first been hard to understand now took shape and became clearer, more useful to me.

I have found that there appear to be several important factors which influence how people will experience loneliness, its degree of intensity and character, and what it represents to them. Separate but interrelated factors are a kind of *Loneliness Barometer*. People experiencing the severest and most inhibiting degree of loneliness generally encounter a greater number and more degree of these characteristics, than do those who have less acute cases of loneliness. More troubled people generally see less hope for working out their unhappy situations since they are more likely to feel a greater degree of hopelessness about themselves and their futures.

Two things particularly stand out in regard to these barometers of loneliness. First: although some lonely people do not exhibit the majority of these characteristics, most do. Secondly: in a great number of cases, high degrees of self doubt and rejection appear most commonly.

1. *Low self-esteem* - leading to fear of failure, fear of trying, fear of being alone, and sometimes even fear of succeeding.
2. *High degree of difference between what is wanted or expected and what they feel they have.*

3. *High degree of self-blame* - feel the "failure" lies with some deficiency inside of them. (#2 and #3 ranked almost side by side.)

4. *Inability to look at themselves honestly* - with humor, with candor and with compassion.

5. *Loss of Control* - feeling that they are powerless to direct, stop, or change things. Afraid of being swept away or pushed into things they don't want to do or be. "If I try this and it doesn't work, things may get out of hand completely."

6. *Strong feelings that their happiness comes from outside them, from other people* - "Without him I am nothing." "When I lost her, I lost a part of myself." "I'll be happier when my husband treats me better."

7. *Inability to connect the events that went before to what is happening now.* "I felt the bastard left me for no good reason! If he'd had a reason, I wouldn't be taking it so bad. We were great together." It is difficult for them to grasp that their lives are not controlled by omnipotent forces, but by behaviors and choices they themselves make. (By this same token, they have trouble seeing themselves connecting in any positive way with a future they can shape.)

8. *Lost sense of masterful identity* - sense of self not clearly defined, certainly not the identity they wished to experience. Do not feel in touch with their idealized "hero" self that was to be spontaneous or creative, or gentle and yet strong, willing to venture out, etc.,—the part of them that dreams dreams and sees the world as open to them. They have retreated to a position of safety rather than challenge.

9. *Inability to accept change* — always searching for a *constant*. Seeing change as fearful. Such individual are often unaware that they have options or

choices, and if they did, would be afraid to give up habits even though they are: "We've fought like cats and dogs since I slipped the ring on her finger, and I guess we ain't going to change now!"

"I know Fred needs to get out. I know it bad, but I don't want to see it. I need him too much myself."

10. *Fixation of thought* - tendency to get stuck with one idea only. Pre-occupation with narrow focus and "tunnel vision" with regard to total problem. Like the story of the man who came to a clinic saying he felt he was now dead. He really could not understand why he was still walking around and had come to find out why that was. The young intern on duty took his finger and pricked it with a needle. Looking down at his own blood, the man said, "I'll be darned, dead men DO bleed!"

11. *Fearfulness, with a tendency to focus on the worst possible outcome—to "catastrophise"* and blow things up and out of proportion. The Sword of Damocles always seems to be hanging over their heads.

12. *Tendency to experience things more on an (emotional) feeling level.* Dwelling on the present emotional feelings rather than turning their attention on solutions and/or making their rational needs known.

13. *Problems dealing with the passage of time*— want control over time. These people view time as leaving them at the starting gate. Would like it to stand still so they could control or recapture the past, or at least bring it along. High degree of rumination about what is lost, the past and the future, their own death, but having difficulty enjoying the living in the present. Trouble viewing the present as a healthy platform upon which to anticipate a bright future.

I did not add a 14th category, *Anger*, although it might

have been appropriate. Anger did not stand out as clearly as the other factors. This may be partly due to the difficulty people have allowing themselves to admit to anger. Many people who are lonely appear to be dealing with various forms of anger which is either turned inward against themselves for their situation, or is turned outward against others seem responsible for their loneliness.

Loneliness Is a Matter of Self-Perception

I believe that you can gather from the issues pointed out in this list that the way *loneliness is experienced is determined by what a person perceives, and on the basis of this, how they interpret their situation.*

If you are lonely right now, how many of the factors I have named apply to you? My guess is all of us would admit to one or two. However, the question really is this: Can we strip away pretense, allow ourselves to review each one honestly and then choose to do something about what we find? And if so, how?

Finally on deep reflection, I realized that the people I had been talking with over the years emphasized how the loneliness effected their personal feelings and particularly their perceptions about themselves. Yet other researchers who are writing about loneliness, highlight the need to get back into the social mainstream of life. The emphasis is on the benefit derived from finding other people to be with. However, there is little or no mention of those factors which keep lonely people from becoming involved with others, and even less mention of how one gets "unstuck."

I suggest we need a change of perspective to do this. We need a down-to-earth, usable way of conceptualizing what's happening and what we might do about it. All of the issues that we are talking about relate in some meaningful way to our *perception* of ourselves, and our place in the order of things. Often these perceptions are colored by factors which we either are not aware of, or don't understand.

One of our problems is that most of us have grown up looking at our behaviors and our motivations from the set perspective we learned as school children, namely that some outside stimulus leads us to a response, and so we are often left waiting for that special stimulus before we feel we can behaviorally respond in a way that gets us what we need. And there is nothing worse than idle waiting, because it often means we've accepted being dependent. And caught in the midst of loneliness, the most terrible thing that can happen to us is nothing.

What if we changed all this? Suppose we look at the problem the other way around. I suggest that *the majority of the lonely people I have experienced live with an unresolved contradiction that I see as a major characteristic of loneliness.* They can never match up their perception of their very real unhappy present life with their idealized views of the past, the present or the future. It is these unmet expectations that lonely people must deal with, because it leaves them feeling unsatisfied, incomplete and susceptible to the depressive lacuna of loneliness.

I have said that we can best begin to cope with loneliness when we change our perspective of it.

Two initial steps are:

1. To accept loneliness as an integral part of being human.
2. To consider how behavior affects our perception of things.

The first step includes forgiving yourself for not being perfect.

The second step may take less time but can be equally rewarding.

Let us assume that *perception* is at the center of our existence. Perception is the sensor, or mirror by which we experience everything going on inside and outside of us. Our value judgments of what is real and what is not are made in terms of all the incoming data which is received and processed in our brain.

In this conceptualization is the idea that each WHOLE PERSON, with all of his/her attributes, personality, faults, etc., strives to reach the highest personal goals which are possible in life. If we set a goal that is clearly unreachable, we are going to end up with a wide difference (or distance) between what we had hoped for and what we believe we get. The degree to which the gap remains open, we will simply refer to as Difference.

The following diagram applies this concept to loneliness:

LONELINESS CONTINUUM

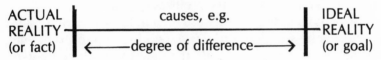

The degree of difference in our perceptions can be seen to expand or contract along the Loneliness Continuum. Our lives are directed towards bringing these two realities together and the further apart they are, the greater is our discomfort. We have said that two factors determining the intensity of the loneliness experience are:

1. The amount of difference between the two realities, and

2. Our assessment of our own responsibility in not meeting these goals.

I can certainly understand better now the frequent disillusionments that I carried in my head as a boy. My expectation ranged from absolute belief in my becoming a famous playwright, cowboy, high-wire artist, racing car driver, etc., to believing that when I grew up, I would be a Mohegan Indian. I never did really figure out how to truly look like an Indian. Anyway, I remained just a boy for a few more years, and then, in spite of myself, grew up. But when we remain lonely, we grow up only physically, because time seems to be leaving our desires behind.

Managing Loneliness

What does the loneliness diagram have to do with managing loneliness? It has everything to do with it, because the perceptual gap created in *finding* ourselves lonely, when our goals were set on un-loneliness, is the source of our pain. A good example of this is when we have a notion somehow that a *normal* happy existence is a life with no loneliness it it. We try to reach that ideal and the equation we come up with is that since we are lonely we're abnormal. That's the misperception, and in order to close the difference and feel better, we've got to bring the hoped-for reality and actual reality closer together.

Two concepts of reality are seen in the world of Richard Price as he sits down to write, pen in hand, or to dictate, tape recorder ready. Ideally the pen moves along by itself and he doesn't have to do anything. He thinks that's the way all writing is, someone who can really write just sits down and does it. But this is not always the case. And what I'm suggesting is that *actual reality* and idealized reality are very different. The difference of perception here is rather large because the idealized version is what Dick Price would like it to be, but the real world is a place where he has to hold a sweaty pencil and write, erase, revise, cross out and work over and over, and to keep changing his composition until it says what he wants it to say. It's not going to write itself.

What I am saying is that so many people either have unrealistic goals or goals they don't know how to arrive at. In terms of loneliness, they may have a goal of unloneliness; but they often do not know how to start the process.

One woman who comes to see me now and then has been lonely and depressed for some time. She feels like staying home in bed because she feels so unworthy. She feels that she is such a poor example of life that nobody is going to want to go near her, so the best thing to do is to stay home. Where it's safe, where she can withdraw and no one will bother her and she won't bother anyone else. In fact, she feels so unworthy, or so useless, that she doesn't feel she deserves to be out in that world with all those "together" people. Also, she fears that she might be rejected if she goes out into that real world.

This woman has a severe problem. If she could evaluate herself on our continuum, there are several ways she might intervene on her own behalf. The first, and most important step she must take is to recognize that change *is* possible. She may believe, as I think many people do, that her loneliness controls her. She may not realize that her earlier expectations were unrealistically high; that if she looked more honestly at where she was on the Loneliness Continuum, she would see that she can either lower her sights or try new ways to change her present reality. She could be kinder to herself and give herself the same sympathy she might give to anyone else who suffered. There are any number of alternatives which might close the painful gap between her unfulfilled, unrealistic self expectations and a more fulfilling lifestyle.

As another step in looking at the causes of loneliness and how our *perception* of it affects its quality and course, I would like to offer one example of how the thirteen factors we have been reviewing operate in real life.

Vincent and I met on a lazy Sunday morning in May at a cemetery. The meeting was totally unexpected. Vin saw me a split second before I saw him. He had just finished scrawling a message across one of the largest headstones he could find. The message read, *"Fuck You, Ms. Cummings!"* Obviously he hadn't expected me to turn up. Behind the shock of surprise in those little boy eyes was the same look I had seen there in other lonely people. He was a sweet, sad kid, similar to youths you see so often in the out-patient departments of mental health centers, referred by the schools, brought by mothers, the kind of kid whose fathers are just not around or are always "too busy" to be available.

"Hi, Vin," I said lamely, realizing that I had interrupted some symbolic kind of affirming action.

"Hi, Dr. Price . . . Dick." A wistful smile crept into the edges of his lips. As I looked down at this little boy, he seemed ancient, "street-wise," and charming—all at ten years old.

"I hate her," he said simply, assuming that I had read his declaration. "She makes me lonely."

"Makes you lonely?" I queried, thinking instantly that I was taking up my role as his therapist again. Vin looked at me earnestly and I felt once more the pain that lay behind his words.

"Yeah, Ms. Cummings is my teacher," he said plaintively, rolling the "mszzz" sound through his teeth. "I used to be her favorite. I try so hard to read but everyone has a gold star but me. She doesn't give me enough time. Some kids have a lot of gold stars. Nobody likes me. She yells at me even when I'm not bad. Am I bad? I never have anyone to play with." There was a long pause, finally he said, "Remember when I used to play Superman?"

Vin tried not to let the tears out, the eyes blinking unsuccessfully. "So, she makes me lonely," he stated again, as though that was all that was needed to convince me. And it was. I believed him, for I saw in him that lonely state that I had once experienced in my own solitary boyhood—his behavior mirrored his unhappy feelings about himself.

Vin was in that emotional state many adults are. He felt sad and helpless about his deteriorating relationship with the friends who he once thought had looked up to him. Also, Vin desperately longed for his teacher's approval. She seemed to him to be the cause of his lonely feelings. He perceived himself as isolated and unlikable, no longer the favorite of the people who were important to him. The present filtered through his experience confirmed his sense of loss, the loss of control over his future, the loss of people's approval, and the subsequent loss of self-esteem. Unanswered questions to himself, and to me, hung heavily around his neck. His psychic energy was invested in the emotional "catastrophe" he was experiencing, and it was channeled partly into negative devaluing and frustration which left no immediate energy to look at the options still open to him.

In a way, Vin's loneliness included the loss of the hero part of his idealized self. In those three words, "Am I bad?" he did what is so characteristic of lonely people everywhere; he conceptualized himself as flawed. His perception was that his feelings were outside of his control. He really wanted, but could not turn back the hands of time to regain the friendships lost before this episode. Vin dreaded his future and saw his present as bleak. He was filled by his fear of isolation.

I knew enough about Vin to admire his spunk at times, in the face of the way his life had been going; so I was glad that at least he was not so wrapped up in self-blame as he was in anger at this point. He had, in his own view, tried hard, and was somewhat aware of the cause and relationship issues he was dealing with. There may have been a bit of denial in Vin's handling of his situation. For instance he rationalized that his teacher was responsible for his actions. But I think that even at his age level, he might have had a sneaking suspicion that nothing really happens in isolation, that each action or reaction creates a chain of new circumstances which again affects further reactions. Still, the discrepancy between Vincent's goals and what he perceived to be his reality, left the wide margin of *difference* which led to his unhappiness.

There is a philosophical quality to my experience of Vin. Perhaps it is because I am so touched by him and by the sensitivity to existential issues in life that his statements generate in me. Perhaps, too, I identify with his metaphors, his myth. I am struck with how clearly Vin's own story highlights the three universal themes which I see being played out over and over in the personal drama of people's own separate loneliness. These are motifs that together constitute a more philosophical than psychological view of Woman/Man. In fact, the three themes that I will enlarge upon are implicitly included within the thirteen factors that I have outlined and comprise an interesting sophical/psychological blend.

Vin and I, and perhaps you, are similar in the way these motifs have affected our lives. It is hard to pinpoint exactly when in my life I began to believe in heroes. When I was younger, I believed that I had all the time in the world to become a hero myself. As a child, I saw simple solutions to complex problems. I believed very strongly that if you were "good" and "true," life would reward you eventually. I did not think of myself as unrealistic for I was convinced tht heroes were fated to overcome the solitary isolation from which they usually seemed to start.

As a child, like Vin, I hungered for the lost language with which to communicate who I was. I searched for a Hero— and for some parenting human being, some body of belief which I could call truth, something I could follow. At first I felt the need to recapture that part of my past that had slipped away. I hoped to somehow find, hold it, and see what was never visible. Perhaps I wanted only what we all want, something immutable, something that would never change and that I could count on.

So, I searched for a Constant that would not fail me. At times I found it in other people whom I had learned to trust; gradually I came to see that it was within me too. I gave up the search for my natural parents at an early age because I discovered that, much as I wanted to, I could not stop or reverse the arc of time. I could not control Time in order to bring them back, and in fact, by letting go, I found other valuable people to love. I realized that permanence is a relative thing and that the hero in me, in quest of identity, would have to accept the principle of change and learn to use it. Sometimes I would even have to let things go in order to be free.

At the core of my own loneliness, I found something special. I finally did not have to run way—not only from loneliness, but from facing who I was.

I think again of my ten-year-old friend, Vin. His behavior was an attempt to bring his perception of being a failure more in line with his idealized goal of perceiving himself ʳful, lovable, and in control of his life. The stimulus for his disruptive, clowning around, "acting out" class-room behavior wasn't just because of poor grades. His behavior concentrated on an attempt to bring about an inner view of himself as being like everybody else, gener-ally successful, and in control of life. His actions then, were an attempt to bring his actual perception more in line with his desired one. These actions, however, were not the ones his teacher wanted. Her hopes were focused on his doing good school work and she misjudged his real desires, i.e., that it was his status among his peers, plus affection that he was hungry for. Their ideas were miles apart. She said, "I know you can do better work and will feel better if you will only try," while inside, he was floundering and controlling his behavior desperately in the only way he knew to reach out for the acceptance he needed.

Vin and his teacher are classical examples of the well-intentioned advice-giver missing the underlying issues in such a way that their advice heightens rather than dim-inishes the other person's sense of helplessness. She was unable to stimulate him towards his idea of success be-cause he had already established in his mind a picture of something different. At this point, there was little chance of positive response.

The small successes of many maladjusted, lonely people depend on where on the continuum they are. If their self-image is poor and they are afraid of being hurt, they may feel that the only way not to be hurt further is not to involve themselves. So what they do is, withdraw further. But somehow, they have to take a tentative step to re-entering the world, one that will give them the confidence to try once more to find the solutions in themselves. For ex-ample, by beginning to evaluate their state with as much personal honesty as possible:

1. Which of the thirteen factors they find most charac-teristic of them.
2. Where they are now in their lives.

3. How they think they got there.

4. Where they would realistically like to be.

5. What talents, contacts. (Even though they may start by saying "Nothing.")

6. What first steps they could begin taking that will make them feel better than they did before.

7. What are the next steps, etc.?

8. Are they willing to back these up with specific actions?

9. If so, when? How?

10. What "back-up" (contingency) plan can be instituted if these first steps are not meeting their needs?

Lonely people might begin by sharing some part of their process with someone else, a friend, a counselor, a self-help group, a minister or religious leader, someone who might say to them, "Well, the first step is: take a risk. Take a step, come out. I care enough about you and here I am. I'm talking to you, here is a piece of reality, this is real. I'm listening to you." But, if you are the lonely person and I'm the person you have chosen to talk to, you might say, "I can't," and so you test me, and you tell me all this terrible garbage about yourself and you go on telling me what a terrible person you are. And then I say, "O.K., that's fine, I hear you." So a little piece of reality gets inserted. The lonely person then can begin to move along the continuum and keep getting closer to other people and a better future, but they will keep testing all the time. But if they find that here is possibly another person, and then another, who can respond to them and who says, "Boy, I've felt that same way myself." They begin to share together. They are moving along a life line. The space that is still in the middle is that difference in perception and the only thing that closes in this gap is *Reality*. Their reality testing helps them find out what the real world is like.

Every once in a while the lonely person runs into rejections or failures or their own stupidity, and they quaver a

bit, and the gap widens momentarily again, because somebody reacts to them exactly the way they imagined everybody would, because of their low self-esteem. At these
times their confidence gets shaken again, and you might be
able to help them inject some more reality.

Another factor to be considered is how difficult it is for
lonely people to realize how purely subjective their feelings are. For example: Walk down any street. Look into the
eyes of the people walking toward you. What do you see?
Indifference? Friendliness? Cautious avoidance? Loneliness? Of course it won't always be the same, but we each
interpret the meaning in those eyes in terms of our own
personal experience, and it probably tells us more about
ourselves than it does about them.

Think about these words for a moment:

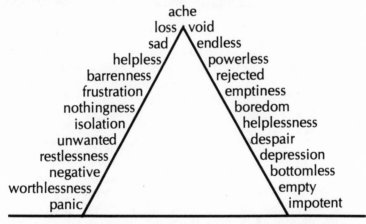

(I do not intend to imply any hierarchy of feelings here)

Twenty-five people (nine men - sixteen women) in my
study offered the definitions surrounding the pyramid in
answer to my question of what one word most symbolized
the experience of loneliness for them. You may wish to add
your own words to this pyramid. Notice how many of these
words indicate poor self images. Such words as : "helpless" - "unwanted" - "sad" - "powerless."

Over a period of time I have become adept at matching a
person's word choices with that person's degree of nega-

tive loneliness. Someone using the word "restlessness," for example, may be only slightly affected, while another person choosing a word implying an extreme such as "bottomless" seems to experience loneliness with a much greater negative impact. The more extreme pain the descriptive words convey, the more helpless the person usually feels. This person's negative feelings of self worth usually intensify with time's passage. So, the words become useful clues to where corrective action can begin.

When we are hurting it is difficult to see the positive side of things. Suppose we know intellectually that almost everything that we can conceptualize has its known opposite. Bad/Good - Heaven/Hell - Man/Woman. If we think about the words in our diagram, and take each one separately and totally reverse its subjective meaning, we can then find its diametric opposite. My opposites go like this:

Meditate on these words for a moment. Become aware of feelings that these new words generate.

Do you feel a shift in your own energy flow? Notice the base line that completes this second pyramid. Let's assume that it represents a line of balance which supports most of those significant values to which we all aspire. Now let's

add our first pyramid to this one, keeping our line of
balance running between the two polarities.

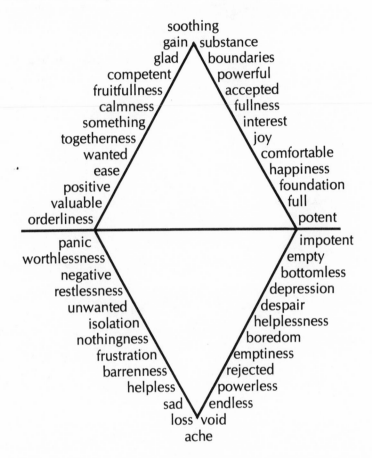

From the configuration, I can visualize two things. One
is a mirror. The other is the difference in my own inner
feelings as I read the words in the upper half as opposed to
my feelings reading the words in the lower half.

Our concept of self is acutely felt at every point of personal crisis, and loneliness is no exception. The words
each of us chooses in expressing loneliness symbolizes a
basic feeling from our past, this past legacy has a mirror

effect upon us in the present. Being able to stop and clearly look at the opposite side of our own negativity is an important tool for recovery. It gives us a contrasting view of loneliness as well as providing a balanced platform to build upon when acute loneliness strikes us. In seeing different possibilities for future and present feelings we can begin to restructure our self-perception and our self-image.

EIGHT

A SEPARATE EXPERIENCE?

. . . . I rememember, I was thinking about the similarities between men and women . . . . men's and women's bodies for example. I was stretched out soaking in the bath tub. It was one of those big, old-fashioned kind, you know, and I was noticing how when I pushed my penis way down between my legs where I couldn't see it, my body had that same lovely moundy, "mons" area that a woman's has.

I kept thinking how much the same we are in so many ways, and yet, I think men are mostly afraid to look at the similarities.

Here we are, each of us with a probable seventy-year lifetime warranty if we just take care of these distinctive bodies of ours. Like it or not, we learn to experience the tremendous influence our separate sexual identities play in our struggle not to be lonely. The relationship of our separate genders to the socially influenced sex-roles we each adopt have a direct and distinct relationship to lonely feelings and are an expression oriented to our environment at a given moment in time.

The cards are stacked from the start: baby girls are most often dressed in pink; baby boys in blue. These are the first symbols of the obvious and intriguing differences in "female/male" physiology; size, shape, strength, function, etc.

Not long ago, you and I used words like "mothering," or "fathering," and felt quite clear about what they meant. It's harder now to define correct roles and images. Qualities of "motherliness" still generally bring to mind images of being tender, holding, comforting, nurturing, perhaps even passively patient and accepting. However, you don't actually have to be a mother to be "motherly"; men can have mothering qualities as can some women. Anthropologist Margaret Mead emphasizes this egalitarianism in illustrating the results of her study of child-rearing practices among people of different cultures. She surmises that the capacity to nurture and raise children is not biologically determined but is a learned response to functions which are assigned to meet the needs of each particular group. These qualities then are not inherent characteristics of women any more than of men.

I have a strong feeling that a parallel situation exists when we compare the effect that our "female" or "male" sexual identities have in relation to how loneliness is experienced. Social influences affect us at every stage; often the paths that lead each of us toward or away from loneliness are largely socially influenced and sanctioned. (This is also true, I believe, of the way that over our lifetimes we each develop ways of defending ourselves and coping, and it influences the amount of self-esteem we bring forward into the moment.)

When I first began studying loneliness I underrated the power of social taboos in creating fears of appearing less than "normal." "Normal" largely means you conform to the "appropriate" sex-role behaviors expected of "well-adjusted" men and women even when pressures to conform sometimes conflict with other intense feelings.

I learned as a boy that I was "not supposed" to feel certain emotions, so I hid them. I never wondered, for example, why the girls my sister's age played with their

dolls in their homes while we boys roughhoused and com-
peted in our games along the street. There was no reason
for confusion as to where one had to fit if one were a normal
boy or girl. I mostly enjoyed boys play, although in retro-
spect I realize also that girl play allowed them to express
their *emotionality*, and their *dreams*, while ours were an
outlet for physical energy. I believe that everyone needs
play therapy with others. The very quality of our lives
hinges on the degree to which we keep learning not to be
afraid to express emotions to others, and to experience
them ourselves. Each of us learns this differently, and in
relation to our sense of sexual identity.

There are some natural gender doubts which are a part of
life, I think. Most of us experience crazy, unrelated
thoughts that seem to pass through the secret closets of our
minds. Those wild, unexpected things sometimes don't
make sense, and sometimes do, or we're scared that they
do?

I was thinking about this the other morning while I was
out running. I had no particular agenda on my mind when I
left the house, but by the time I was several miles down the
road I was experiencing a kind of kaleidoscope of ideas
flashing through my mind.

One of these was the thought that it would be unfortunate if women did not have the same preoccupation with
sexuality as men. Here I was running along and recalling
an ad that I had seen in a magazine. The ad showed several
pictures. One was a photograph of an attractive woman
wearing a lacey bra sold by the advertiser. Another was a
drawing of a woman wearing the bra in which just a little
bit of her nipple bulge was noticeable in profile. In the
third picture of the advertiser's bra, there was no seductive
bulge at all. The ad described how their bras had the
natural look, and intimated that the hidden nipple was
subtly attractive.

And here I was, days later, thinking of the pictures. I
thought there was something lovely about that nipple's
shape. And as I ran along I wondered to myself if other

people had these thoughts too. We can't often tell each other these things, can we? And yet, that is just what I am trying to do. And I don't see my involvement with this story as a sexist thing at all, because it comes from appreciation for the human form.

It gives a kind of spice to life, doesn't it, to appreciate sexual identity, to respect and enjoy it?

Some time ago, one wonderful moonlight night along the Big Sur of California, I participated in an Arica group evening of meditations and dancing. As the stars came out, we moved onto a large, open veranda overlooking the ocean and began to free dance to the rhythmic accompaniment of African drums, violins and hammer-on-dulcimers. I remember feeling both enormously beautiful and enormously loving that night. I lost myself completely in that dancing and gave myself over to the "free-spirit child" in me. It was like a fusion of creative energy blending with the warmth of being part of those people at that time and place. The crucial shock came later that evening. It was at the exact moment when I had felt the most extended, fluid and graceful in my dancing. In my mind I had become one with all of the great ballet dancers of the world, floating endlessly, it seemed, at the top of my leaps. Suddenly, a quick shiver of awareness ran through me. I was noticeably conscious of the exquisitely delicate extension of my fingers, and the "feminine" mannerism of my dancing at that moment. In that split, indecisive instant, I felt a flush of embarrassment, and then, because at the same time I somehow knew that this was also a rich part of me. I continued dancing. However, I will never forget how that cultural taboo against men's appearing "feminine" affected this expressive part of me.

I see this creative expressive aspect of men's personality as one they are having a hard time reconciling with the traditional macho concept of manhood. Allowing all parts of one's character to come out has to do with being centered, and the centering I am speaking of is learning to live in a way that we are not afraid to be genuinely in touch with the three aspects of our experience we call

Thoughts - our reasoning process which involves thinking, deciding, describing, knowing

Feelings - our emotions and sensations

Behavior - our actions we carry out in the environment.

Whether or not these characteristics meet conventional standards of gender identity, as adults, we cannot deny or refuse to take responsibility for these aspects of ourselves for long without creating either internal or external repercussions. There are times when our *feelings* produce anxiety and we would like to run away from them or disown them. Such a subterfuge will not work. It is unhealthy for us to try to escape our own feelings because even if we succeed we lose the balanced perspective of what we are doing and experiencing. When we are able to allow those three aspects of ourselves we try to hide to surface we have our minds and our bodies *centered* in reality. No side of our nature is closed off, distorted, or unconnected. We can experience ourselves and other things fully. I believe that the effects of being centered, or not being centered, apply to everything that we have been talking about in terms of men, women, and loneliness.

If you are man, you often begin the struggle not to be lonely with a problem of whom you can confide in or express yourself to. Feelings of self-doubt, physical vulnerability or emotional weakness are "not appropriate" in a society which has prized "masculinity" for centuries and equated it with traits of assertiveness, strength, denial of fear, and the acquisition of possessions. At the same time, the game of life where there always seem to be winners and "losers," less valued traits of emotionality, concern with domestic affairs, gentleness, receptivity, are seen as more characteristic of "feminity." A major distinction appears to be the opposition between *passivity*, equated with weakness, losing and women on the one hand, and *activ-*

ity, equated with winning and men on the other. This stereotypical thinking finds expression in the view of a woman's participation in sex, for example, as being passive and receptive, women "letting themselves be loved," while men are seen as active and "making love." These stereotypes are not necessarily put-downs but in most cases, I think they really are. Anything that opens us to a sense of helplessness disables our self esteem. To many people, the marriage vows imply "you belong to me," which underneath often means, "I must hold on to you for fear that I will be left alone." This is reinforced by the double standard, where the woman is supposed to feel proud and protected when her husband or lover is possessive and strong. However, if she becomes the possessive or strong one, she is liable to be labeled as "bitchy" and undermining to the male position.

Such stereotyping places a female in some conflict with strong, assertive values. She must often look for self-acceptance according to masculine-imposed standards, either by competing with men on their terms or by seeking the gratifications of child rearing and home life which are seen as special to her. Too often she ends up having to make a choice between one or the other. Consequently, she is left with a sense of incompleteness, because, either choice she makes she perceives herself as functioning in a devalued position. Let me point up this business of devaluation by sharing with you a conversation that a co-worker of mine reports having:

"A friend said to me how difficult it was for her to make a phone call, to reach out to a man. She said 'You know, I think that it gets harder the older you get, maybe it's self-protection. Somehow, when I was in school and college and so on, it was no problem. I could call a guy and that was it. It was a whole different kind of thing. I'm still under forty, but it's getting harder. I suspect that society makes things harder. A woman has a feeling that she is putting herself down because she has to make overtures to the man. It's as if she's subjecting herself, suggesting a submissive kind of relationship that probably has to do with the use of her body. And she doesn't want to be demeaned in that way. That is the feeling I think a lot of women who are divorced experience. When guys call them, many women feel men expect sex and many men feel, here's a woman who's divorced, and she needs sex, so I can give it to her. I've heard this description from many divorced women. Married men will even call them. Men that they knew casually before make crude sexual advances. The woman make choices to protect themselves by saying, well, this one is less worthy, and that one is something else. I don't know."'

How do you advise someone in situations like this? I keep asking myself. I suspect that what people usually recommend like my friend is to join groups, or go to a bar, or the usual places where you can meet people. I suspect what happens in nine out of ten cases is that the lonely go and don't meet anybody, and it just reinforces the feeling that there's something wrong with them. First, because they had to force themselves to act, and second, because having done this, they were rejected again.

I told my friend about a woman with whom I worked who felt that she was a real nothing. Her husband was always putting her down. Finally his negative opinion of her as a nothing became her own. He kept reinforcing it over and over again. When she finally broke out of that "stay-home-and-get-worked-over-the-coals-cycle" and found another scene where people didn't know her history and began treating her kindly because of all the good things that she had to offer, she began getting stronger. She still had trouble at home, but as she found strength in the outside world, it made it easier for her to deal with negativity at home. "You have to get validated wherever you can get validated, and build from there, so that you are then able to face the situation where you felt the worst," is her own analysis.

How do such choices affect a woman's susceptibility to

loneliness? We have said that how you feel about yourself is a major factor in where you find yourself on the Loneliness Continuum. Small wonder that many women are lonely and depressed, since they are missing something that they may never have had—a positive image of themselves.

Consider my friend, Paula Belton. Her husband, Tom, "heads up" their family and is confused when Paula says that she has trouble being her own person. She tells him she seldom sees herself when she looks into her mirror. What she sees there is a woman who is so busy trying to assume her expected role of family "housekeeper," "wife," "mother," that she cannot find herself anymore.

Tom is different. In some ways I think he represents that imaginary tall and confident universal man you see leaning against so many cars along so many streets in so many towns across America. Tom is a man who pictures himself as something other than what he is. Since he does not really draw full pleasure from being with his wife and children in a sharing, family way, he longs for something more exciting "out there" which he is not quite able to define and which seems always elusively just out of reach.

Although I think Paula is more down-to-earth practical than Tom, and less apt to deceive herself, she partially understands Tom's need for fantasizing. Like many other women that I have interviewed, Paula knows what lies ahead and what is more, at age fifty-three, she recognizes and feeds on her growing resentment that her own dreams and aspirations, like her mother's before her, have never been as valued in this society as her husband's. Understandably, she recognizes that women have had less opportunity to learn independence within the home and therefore have had more cause to feel immobilized and dependent.

During a discussion with Paula about how women and men approach loneliness, I mentioned how fascinated I was with many people's observations that men often appear to be the "active" initiators of intimate relationships, while women tend to be the "reactive" maintainers of these relationships. Paula merely glanced over at me for a moment with those wonderful eyes that seem to contain an endless well of compassion and understanding, and then shrugged her shoulders, as though in agreement.

A few days later, Paula's delayed response came back to me in the form of this note. Although she generalizes these issues, I know that she speaks first for herself:

". . . We all come naked into the world . . . At his worst Man has always had the capacity to cow, over-power, and exploit Woman. At his best Man has always had the capacity to value, protect, and honor women. . . Men are apt to be aggressive, adventurous and logical. Women are apt to be passive, home-oriented, wily.

"The differences carry over into the area of the loneliness experience. The lonely girl or woman almost always has romance on her mind. Romance first, sex second. One suspects that it is the reverse for the lonely man . . .

"Women develop a terrible patience in the face of loneliness. Men want to rush off and do something—get drunk, find a sex partner, drive a car, play or watch a sport, make some money, and so on . . .

"Women will grin and bear it more docilely, busy-ing themselves with more passive occupations. Many women find much solace in their maternal or nurtur-ing instincts as mothers or perhaps as medical pro-fessionals, etc.

"Women tend to worry more and to refuse to relin-quish their worries. They worry about real situations and imaginary situations almost equally. They worry not only about themselves but others close to them. Women cry a lot more than men, which is supposed to be a healthy response. I suggest that crying is a symp-tom of frustration and that women suffer a dispropor-tionate amount of frustration because it really is a 'man's world' . . .

"There is currently a tremendous new wave of sex-ual freedom going on. Women are supposed to benefit

from this. But do they? Society has always had pro-
miscuous women. Society has always had prostitutes.
But such women were not typical. I consider that the
ordinary woman of today is not much different from
her ancestors, and that indiscriminate use of sex is
anathema to her, and leads to a desperate loneliness.

"Prayers come more easily to the lips of women
than to men. Perhaps such expressions are the reactions to the experience of loneliness, rather than positive actions in the direction of a deep spiritual
quest. . .

"Women take more comfort from the simple act of
talking than men do. Female children tend to talk
earlier, develop better vocabularies, and tend to
manipulate their particular social situations verbally
rather than physically. When lonely women seek out
someone to talk to they have less pride than men do in
admitting to loneliness, to weakness, to misgivings of
one sort or another. When men are driven to confide
their troubles, they reserve the right to salvage some
sense of masculine pride from the experience.
Women don't have that hang-up. . .

"All this is not to say that women react to loneliness in more noble and virtuous ways than men do.
Many women are self-destructive, using and abus-
ing alcohol and other drugs. Many women become
mean-spirited and degenerate into gossipy trouble-
makers. Many women allow their minds to deter-
iorate and settle for soap operas, bingo, and trashy
periodicals. Women are no more saints than men
are. We are different, but perhaps equals in our
capacity or incapacity to handle loneliness in positive ways."

It's Often Harder for Men to Admit to Deeper Emotions

Paula's note touches briefly on another aspect of difference that I believe shapes some of our paths towards or
away from loneliness. I am quite aware of the contrasting
differences beween Paula's female upbringing and my

masculine one. For one thing, I have always been encouraged to be more physically aggressive than she was. I think that most men develop a kind of "motor mindedness," or ability to travel and extend physical horizons more actively than women do. We are pushed by parental, environmental and cultural mores to develop tools to cope with the stress of this activeness. These include the ability of not openly submitting to defeat, sadness or resignation, and especially not to tears.

Supposedly, the gender stresses of boyhood/manhood lead towards developing a healthy capacity to deal with problems, and in a way they do, but not necessarily with problems of an emotional nature. Because men are socialized to be strong and not express pain, they often tend to have more difficulty than women in admitting to deeper levels of emotion. Often their more action-oriented behaviors are a defensive substitute against being in touch with their feelings of sadness, pain, loneliness, or confusion. This is one reason I believe that men as a group appear to be less in touch with their emotional selves than women are. Men have been "expected" to handle feelings through action. Women have been "expected" to handle feelings in an emotional passive way. However, the image of the strong, silent male is deceptive, since such men find little comfort in the use of denial or silence. Silence itself does not make pain go away. What happens instead is a gradual erosion of self-confidence, a building-up of inner pressures, and an increasing sense of alienation.

In thinking now about the different ways that our susceptibility to loneliness is affected, I find myself coming up with analogies that I borrow from the sea. There is an aspect of the non-sailor's perception of the sea and a sailor's life which I feel has significant relationship to loneliness in men. This has to do with a central theme of loneliness which is *closeness* and *distance,* and the way that each one of us avoids or approaches social intimacy and responsibility.

Because of social encouragement to be the active, adventurous ones, men in particular are torn between the desire to be, on the one hand, "care-free" and unfettered, like the romantic image of explorers everywhere, and on the other hand, to maintain close ties at home. The lives of many of the professional seamen that I have known and sailed with on ships typify certain aspects of the lonely life, which I find beautifully illustrated by the master's thesis of Robert Davis, titled, *Some Men of the Merchant Marine*. 1907, and quoted by Margaret Woods in the book *Paths of Loneliness*.

> . . . . they did want two things which in general society is associated with: wives and homes. First, they wanted, somewhere a headquarters, and second, they wanted some part of their lives to be connected with women. . . .
>
> They had a craving for a headquarters somewhere along the shore, a place where they could leave their trunk, if they had one; a place to which they could project their minds, wherever they might wander, and visualize the position of the furniture, and imagine just what the inmates of the place were doing at the different hours of the day, a place to which they could send a picture postcard or bring back a curio, a place to which they could always return and be sure of a welcome. . .
>
> They wanted the anchoring power of a home without its responsibilities. . . .
>
> They also had a craving, unconnected with sexual appetite, to be connected with some woman. It is a great thing for a lonely man to occupy the center of a woman's attention. . . .
>
> The seaman, with his yearning for a home and a woman's affection on the one hand, and his desire to be free from the restraining force of these responsibilities on the other hand, is another Ishmael, struggling between two conflicting calls, Sarah's call to tea and the call of the open road. . . .

It is not the seaman's life as such that keeps many of these men lonely, away from home, or psychologically unavailable. It is their unwillingness, or inability to accept the ups, down, and difficulties which a meaningful, in-depth, relationship requires. They avoid the necessity of being totally for and with another person, mutual sharings and the risk of vulnerability.

I think it is also correct that part of *the success of a truly intimate relationship requires a giving of the self, plus the ability to self-disclose and not to hide.* Because men have been conditioned to present an outward appearance of calmness and control, it is often seen as a woman's role to submerge her own individuality and to concentrate on helping men unburden their hidden feelings. Facing experiences honestly is an important step in dealing with loneliness. I have never found a person who was in an intimate and openly sharing relationship with another person who felt lonely while involved in that experience.

Let's look at the antecedents of some of the behaviors that we are talking about here. For example, Tim Collins, a psychiatrist and colleague of mine, sees quite a number of seemingly successful young men and women from top-notch colleges. He describes them as often being very intelligent, having qualities of persistence in getting tasks done, sometimes to the point of being obsessional about it. Often they are the good workers, only they don't become close to people—instead erect a barrier between social conversation and meaningful sharing. Tim reports that initially, they don't define their problems as loneliness, but as time goes on, they begin to say something like, "No matter what I do, I'm bored and it doesn't matter who or what I get close to, I know I'll eventually get bored. Everything always ends this way."

Finally, they will begin to talk about their strong feelings of being disconnected and outside of things. Tim points out that they describe the sensations they experience as those of emptiness.

Some of the men particularly may have all the outward accoutrements of success but inwardly still are feeling hollow and trying to stave off a sense of low self-esteem. At a deeper level these men sometimes appear to fear that their inner emptiness will be detected, if they get too close to other people, and they will be rejected, or, if they are unsuccessful, they may be abandoned. The hallmark of the relationships they form is often a reluctance to get deeply

involved unless they can see a definite return for themselves. It is sad to see these men years later as they try to
cope with their loneliness, perhaps finally wondering why
they hadn't been more available to their families, who they
never really got to know and who never got to know them.

You can see the result of this same underlying insecurity
in the actions of some kinds of lonely women Tim often
speaks about. Some are very narcissistic young women
who want to make conquest of attractive men. These
women enter into a relationship in order to acquire people.
Such a relationship is really feeding of the empty self.
After the sexual conquest, once it is time to really build the
relationship, these women dissolve them, and seek new
people to give them substance and validation. But it
doesn't work, and this kind of woman will come in with
the complaint, "Well, I've been in bed with dozens of guys
and none of it means anything, I'm still lonely."

There are other situations which lead certain women to
express loneliness in different ways from men. Some
women will make their children the focus of their lives. As
this is the most meaningful part of their lives, it will be a
struggle for them when, in late adolescence their children
begin to leave the "nest." The problem for such a woman
then becomes one of filling the loneliness vacuum caused
by her children leaving. Certainly she will be more able to
manage this loss if she can find a substitute. Perhaps it will
be accomplished by becoming involved in certain church
group activities with other women in her neighborhood,
going back to work, or finding something to get involved
in that will gratify her.

My colleague, Tim, also suggests that the Women's
Movement is sometimes addressed to this kind of woman.
It is saying, "Why are you sitting around doing nothing?
Why are you being so dependent on men?" But what
comes through is: "Why are you letting men run your
life?" The Women's Movement proposes that women of all
ages take charge, cultivate more action-oriented, initiative-
taking personalities, and use their capacities for various

kinds of work, which will give them senses of self-esteem.

I think this form of consciousness-raising is useful to many lonely women. Women are being encouraged to move out of the home in the sense of building relationships and connections to life outside the home, so that they can have a greater scope of experience and hopefully a greater degree of gratification in all areas of their lives. The kind of woman who can do this is not looking for her own narcissistic gain, because she's inwardly secure in trusting herself. Whatever loneliness she experiences will probably not be long-lasting.

Men Share the Same Capacity for Loneliness as Women

When you strip away all the camouflage and look honestly at how we all generally function, you still find that men do share the same capacity for feelings, including loneliness, that women do, but they often attempt to adapt by keeping certain levels of emotions hidden more deeply, even from themselves.

When you or I believe that parts of our natural emotionality are seen as "inappropriate" and we hide them from each other (or ourselves), we can be left only with the feeling that a part of us is missing. We have denied an important aspect of our character. "Feminine" characteristics lie dormant in men, just as "masculine" characteristics do in many women, and what is sad is that in this supposedly "let it all hang out" culture, part of ourselves still remain closeted.

This position is doubly damaging because when parts of our natural selves are devalued, then we perceive that we do not have the personal qualities necessary to promote our own happiness and seek our ideal in others. In this way, we play a not-so-neat trick on ourselves and the outcome can only be estrangement.

The men whom I have interviewed and worked with about their feelings of separation and loneliness, seem just

as vulnerable underneath and just as susceptible to feelings of failure or loss as women do. The difference then is
only in *how* men handle feelings in relation to *how* women
handle feelings. My findings indicate to me that *women
and men both share in feelings of loneliness. However,
they come to it via different paths.*

You can see these differences demonstrated in many,
sometimes strange ways, like my own recent participation
in a workshop held at Harvard University, where I was able
to compare notes with my woman companion about graffiti on the walls of the women's and men's rooms. I was
impressed that on the walls of the typical men's rooms in
this bastion of intellectual energy that is called Harvard, I
found more silly, boring and low-class graffiti than in any
place I have ever seen. Dull is the best I can say for it. You
can rate Harvard at the top of the list, however, in terms of
sheer over-abundance of men's room graffiti; it is everywhere. Statements of loneliness? Only indirectly. There
was very little genuine personal feeling commemorated on
those walls. Mostly there were the typical sexual tryst
invitations to "meet me here at so-and-so time," the usual
terrible graphics, bad verse, emphasis on sexual prowess,
organ size, and repititious tattlings, such as "Mary Har-
wick does it free!!!" "Joe blows. . ." etc. Most of these
comments come across as cold or hedonistic. There is a
kind of chilling quality of alienation, separatism and
estrangement screaming from those walls.

Things are often different in the ladies' rooms of the
world, I believe, and Harvard's are no exceptions. Examples of shared feeling, and mutual support can be found
here in abundance. But then, my friend, Ann, like "Kil-
roy," was there and can report on this better than I.

"... women never used to write on the walls like men
did ... it depends on where you are, too, how women
respond to each other's hurt or questions. On one of
the stalls here was the statement, 'I am 4 months
pregnant and I'm afraid to tell my parents. What am I
going to do?' That's just one comment, but there is

writing all over; often somebody makes a comment on what was said and somebody else answers that, and you see the whole wall covered from top to bottom with these statements and counter-statements. There was one statement about a relationship somebody was having with a man and someone else commented, 'The trouble with you is, your whole life depends on a man.' It was a real feminist kind of statement."

Somehow, I feel good when I think about the kind of supporting kinship she is speaking about. As we left arvard, I looked up and saw a sign on the door of one of the buildings which read, "MODERN EDUCATION HAS MOVED TO THE 3RD FLOOR OF THE FRANKLIN UNION." I disagree; modern education has moved much further than that.

I feel that these illustrations of the different ways that men and women handle and express feelings help us to see how different behaviors either help or hinder us in feeling closer and more connected to other people. For example, the men whose graffiti appears all over those walls, and many of the men who have been able to come and talk to me about the pain of the loneliness, have in many ways never discovered (or kept hidden) the necessary vocabulary to put their innermost feelings into words. Without being able to share with other people what we are feeling, we close off possible avenues of intimacy and friendships, or if we maintain relationships, they are on a superficial level. Men have an enormous capacity to play and be competitive with their friends, "buddies," on the golf course, kid around at the bar, but often such superficial meetings are the limit of their closeness with other men, and perhaps with women, too.

In terms of the centering mentioned earlier, it appears to me that those men who can find a closer balance between their emotional and intellectual natures and who are not afraid to move to deeper levels of expressing feelings end up with more substance and intimacy in all their relationships. Emancipated men are not afraid to be authentic.

Women, too, need to find that balance between their rational thinking selves and their emotionality. Often, when people are feeling lonely, they are apt to see only the bad parts of the picture, and there develops a kind of narrowed-down tunnel vision which keeps them from seeing other important aspects of situations in which they are involved.

Changing our perspectives of female/male roles will unfreeze some of our stereotypes. A woman friend of mine expressed this feeling to me.

> ". . . . I think of the ideal female/male relationship as an equal one. For me, it's symbolized in the difference in the typical way people visualize holding hands. The man, for example, expects to enfold the woman's hand, her hand inside, his covering, and around. I see it differently. In a truly successful and sharing relationship, I see the extended open hands of woman and man touching evenly, fingertips touching fingertips with caring, palms touching palms, and neither side dominating."

As we practiced this new kind of touch, I felt everything that she was saying, and I can feel the warmth of that touch to this day. For me, it is impossible to be lonely while I am in any truly honest and sharing situation with anyone. It is only when one or the other of us becomes dishonest, or, if the relationship shifts from a co-equal one to one of dependency or dominance, that feelings of low self-esteem creep in. Although I realized this intellectually, for many, many years, I wish that I personally had understood it all much earlier and with the emotional clarity that I do now.

We usually have some sense and some dream of our potentials, so our struggles and our pleasures in life are reaching for that something we feel is out there, which realistically, we may never quite attain. Personally, I think that one of the most powerful factors in making some of our goals for closeness possible right now comes from women. Men benefit from it too, but I'm not sure that they understand how or appreciate how much. I've been watching closely over the last few years as women have begun to identify more and more with each other as "sisters" and allies in overcoming oppressive female stereotypes and second-rate status. Women are "coming out." They are allowing themselves to explore all aspects of their womanhood, feeling their personal "woman-power," and their uniqueness. There is something very beautiful about this new revolution.

It seems to me that many of the men I have come to know are strangely uneasy about this new-found friendship that women are developing with each other. Numerous men are feeling loneliness themselves in a special way right now, particularly if they are observant. There is something else, too, that men are experiencing and I feel it is akin to jealousy. They are feeling shut out as they watch and hear about women getting together in their consciousness-raising groups and other feminist meetings, finding ways to move from loneliness to relatedness through group association, gaining through the special closeness they are finding with each other. Some of the men I know are attempting to emulate women's successes, but their group efforts are often without the same shared needs that lead women to befriend their sisters.

Women are growing more able now to describe what is happening to them, to describe sexual feelings for example, and to look openly at how men's attitudes have affected their sexual identities. Many women understand that sex isn't the antidote for loneliness that men think it is. Intimacy is much more than physical touching. They wish men could understand this.

I feel that women have sometimes been the recipients of men's unfair anger over sexual issues. I wonder how many women have been accused of being "frigid" or felt themselves to be "impotent" in relationships with men. These are the same words you might hear when people brand their feelings about loneliness. In this regard we are dealing with the sense of non-performance and powerlessness women often feel that finds a parallel in fears of failure and of rejection.

A large number of women reported feeling "empty" in their sexual relationships with men, because they feel used or they experience a feeling that their own needs for tenderness and caring have not been recognized or appreciated. Contrastingly, I would point out that a number of the men with whom I have spoken feel misunderstood by women. They believe women misinterpret their persistence in attempting to establish loving relationships as manipulation. These men see women as bargaining, or tacking on conditions or limitations in order to love. These conditions are, for example, "we can go so far, but no further," or, "if you really loved me, you would put the ring on my finger." There are all kinds of relational oppression and some of these men see women as pushing them "to be successful," so that the woman can own things, keep up with the neighbors, or be compensated for the burden of their "women's lot." Again, feeling *empty* and feeling *lonely* are elements of the anxiety that this kind of unfulfilling relationship often creates.

It has been said that the antidote for loneliness is in relationships. If this is true, and I believe it can be, then we should also recognize that unequal relationships can breed further loneliness, and only balance and true sharing reduce intrinsic loneliness.

The Women's Movement has re-emphasized the phenomenon of *friendship* as a model for relationships. In friendship, we fulfill our needs to belong and yet each of us remains ourselves. In this way the integrity of each person is recognized and preserved. Unlike family relationships, our friendships are chosen freely and are based only on mutual need. The worthwhile friendship model is one of respect, and as such it is not possessive. Relatedness vs. autonomy is a difficult issue to satisfy when we are lonely, because friendships are often chosen because both or one of the parties has unsatisfied needs.

In terms of becoming unlonely then, I feel that growing

numbers of women are on to something important. Certainly they are *choosing* to identify with their potential strength. They do not choose to remain confined, alone, waiting at home. There is, in many small ways, a burst towards freedom. Because of this new phenomenon, women no longer feel the same need to be escorted by men to bars, plays, restaurants, dances, etc. More and more women are enjoying going out to these places with other women, even to strip joints, where the tables are turned, and the strippers now are men. In some female to female relationships, there is the same sense of freedom, of "palling around" that men have enjoyed. This female independence from men is spreading into other aspects of a woman's life, including at times her choice of a female partner for sexual love.

With freedom of choice there is sometimes a different perspective than always believing that an exclusive relationship of itself is the answer to loneliness, particularly if that relationship proves to be an unfulfilling one. Instead of women obsessively needing love relationship they are finding it is much easier to be strong when you are self-reliant and can take care of yourself. Then you can move freely and choose friendships from positions of independence, not weakness.

There is, however, another side to the freedom of choice, the considerable degree of pain and loneliness generated through the uncoupling of those involved in the many temporary living-together relationships of today. It may be easier to get into such a relationship, but it is also easier to get out. There are never any real guarantees in love and in modern times it is less difficult to leave an unfulfilling relationship. Still, a lot of egos are getting bruised in the process.

Despite this drawback, I see positive aspects to a liberation movement as a cure for loneliness. Men and women both can benefit, by discovering reasons to overcome their own damaging inhibitions. What a liberation movement is all about is freedom from oppression, both the inner oppression we place on ourselves and the outer oppression placed upon us, either of which can leave us feeling vulnerable, devalued, worried, alone.

Two things become important here. For one, relationship role changes are in order. Secondly, there is an opening of boundaries formerly reserved for one sex only, as ideal stereotypical sex-role models begin to include a view of women extending their self-expression to pursuits *outside* of the home, and men more *within* the home.

I would not have begun this book if I had not believed that there was something that you and I could learn from experience or that we could do to change the course of our lives.

I find that within the fluctuating rhythms of life a motif emerges. None of us wants to live continually behind drawn curtains, encased in our own personal experience. Our thrust is to enter into and share the life-dreams of others in order to give sustenance to our own. In doing this we are engaged in a sometimes lonely and silent revolution to liberate hidden parts of the self. But we cannot really liberate ourselves without liberating each other. We always come back to *trust*, I think, trusting in our own unique identities and the unique identities of other human beings.

In moving from isolation to connectedness it seems increasingly essential that we move closer to the center of our conciousness—both those "man" and "woman" polarities and the genderless human being ones that exist within us. In acknowledging our identities, we are also making an important social statement. Loneliness, like love, is not a cause, it is a result. When we perceive every woman and man as being equally valuable to the stability and evolution of our society, we will not try to build our own dream at the expense of someone else's.

NINE

GETTING STARTED —: The Hardest Part

> He held her close to him for the first
> time, knowing full well that for him
> to love anybody was a leap into the
> unknown. "But I have to stop run-
> ning," he thought. "I have to belong
> to someone."

You know how serendipitously good ideas sometimes appear? This morning I was sitting at my desk preparing to write. Sunlight from two large south-facing windows streamed into the room and across the blank sheet of paper in front of me. How do I begin today?, I thought.

I had already decided that these last three chapters would be more closely focused on the solutions of loneliness.

As I sat enjoying the warmth of the sunlight I was suddenly aware that our big tiger cat, L'Amico Fritz, who had appeared on our doorstep last winter and stayed on to adopt us (or we him), was inching his way up and into my lap. We are pretty friendly, Fritz and I, and so I said, "That's O.K., Fritz. You and I pals, aren't we? We're just going to sit here and be together." So while Fritz lay purring, I sat reflecting on the quality of our relationship.

Things would have been different if he had not happened by. I would still have enjoyed my solitude tremendously, but his being with me added a dimension that made the experience unique. Just to look at him made me feel good inside. I wanted to put my face against his as a sign of our caring, and I did. In that moment I needed him to experience the same delicious closeness that I was feeling. In sharing the ambience of bonding with L'Amico Fritz, I experienced the essential element for defeating loneliness and finding connectedness.

"Good energy" flowed between us because the antithesis of loneliness is a sense of vitality. In this case, that vitality of feeling was connected with Fritz, and beyond that, was connected with the possibilities inherent in the day, the sunshine warmth, with you, and the writing ahead of me. I said to Fritz, "Here we go, let me try this chapter out on you," and leaning forward carefully so as not to disturb our relatedness I started to write.

There is an essential correlation between knowing something about loneliness and doing something about it—especially since it is the unknown in loneliness that gives it power in the first place. The more that we can understand that the vagrancies of loneliness are largely products of our own mind, the easier it will be to accept loneliness as a phenomenon which is controllable.

I am suggesting that we experience loneliness as an *inner-feeling* but it is largely a *problem of how we think.* If we lose our close friend we recognize that we will miss this person. We can imagine different aspects of life without this person with whom to share them. Perhaps, like children caught in divorce separations, we imagine even that this person left because of something we were not able to do. Our inner speculation and processing possibly causes us to go thrugh various feelings such as anxiety, depression, guilt, or loneliness. It all begins as a result of our mind's sense of what the loss means. And naturally, our mind functions in relation to how we have learned to view ourselves and the world.

The healthy aspect of all this is that we already know that if we can look realistically at the events that are happening to us, and try to understand them without blowing things out of all proportion, we have a good chance of managing to handle our genuine feelings of grief without doing it in a self-defeating way. It is quite natural when our mind recognizes a tragic loss to feel as though a part of us is missing, and that our "heart is broken" as a result. The feelings of pain are simply recognition of how valuable the person has been to us. People who are aging have a more acute awareness of time passing, and of people passing with it. This sensitivity causes us to see material possessions as less important.

When we are alone, or we feel alone and perhaps lonely, there are still choices open to us. We can move towards other people or activities that satisfy us, or, we can remain disengaged and lonely. It does take some courage to make some alterations in our behavior. And it takes *truthfulness* about our own part in why we are unhappy.

In order to overcome the negative ennui which afflicts many lonely people, begin right now to think of and then list the myriad of things that you might do to mobilize yourself to become active and involved in something that would make you less isolated. Stop to consider what kind of assets you possess, skills, techniques, insights, strengths, that you could bring into use as component parts of a LONELINESS SURVIVAL KIT?

To give this suggestion substance that you can hold on, begin by closing your eyes. Imagine now that you are standing naked in the center of a huge field. You are totally alone. Hold this image a moment. Now imagine that you are searching around for the essential implements of your Loneliness Survival Kit. You need them immediately because you feel desolate, or you are afraid that you will be.

However, you cannot seem to find them in the surrounding area. This is because they are inside of you as *beliefs* (and skills). What you have at hand to deal with your lonely feelings is your own power to reason. And then, because beliefs are only made visible through your actions, you can write down alternate actions you might take to alleviate your painful feelings.

When we speak of beliefs as a potent force we are talking of those already-learned tenets which we have adopted and live by—our own moral code; our value system, or more simply, ideas and concepts such as believing that the world is round, stealing is bad, Santa Claus exists. I think that it is useful sometimes to think about what these are and create a diary of your philosophy of life. We all have our own ideas. Some examples might be:

1. I believe wholeheartedly that I find answers, meaning, and satisfactions in life as I learn to solve my own problems and come to understand them.

2. My personal hope for the present and future lies in my willingness to open myself to positive feelings.

3. I must challenge the imaginary dangers that I face —knowing that failure to draw from my own inner resources can lead to loneliness.

4. I go with the belief that my life does make a difference—that the more I can learn to accept myself the more room there will be to accept others in my life.

5. Trust in myself can be regained.

6. I believe it is true that:
      THERE IS NOTHING
      But there is much
   I CAN GIVE YOU
      that, while I cannot give,
   WHICH YOU HAVE NOT
      you can take.
   (From a letter written by Fra Giovanni in 1513)

As we search deeper into our personal Suvival Kit we come to the common things that we may have known about for years and perhaps forgotten, or that people had suggested but at the time they had little import, but now take on meaning. We may have suppressed many of these potential ideas, but they are not lost, if we now search them out and open our minds to them. Like the time that we read the book that suggested we take stock of who our real friends were and why. Or the woman we dated who told us that she liked us better when we were not always so insufferably polite. Or the time that your father pointed out how you characteristically assumed that some of your friends would not want you around, when, in fact, he felt they would enjoy your company. These are examples of retrieved ideas that we can draw upon if we will only stir our subconscious minds a bit and let our natural memoirs emerge.

In one way our Kit is really made up of brief and potentially useful homilies to ourselves. Each one may be only the tiniest pebble dropped on the still waters of a pond. Yet its ripple effect begins a reaction which spreads outward to every segment of our environment.

Using this energy principle, there are some very useful ways that loneliness and its concommitant, depression, can be overcome. I would like to begin with a story that hapened to me.

Not very long ago, I asked two friends of mine who had read what I had written thus far to tell me quite honestly what they felt was still missing for them in these pages. "Tell us more about what *you* learned *from* your loneliness each of them said. Then one of them added, "Don't you see, your answers will be insights for us, too."

Later I realized I had been forming these answers myself for a very long time. I thought again of my response to my friend Marleen's similar request. "How much time have you got?" I responded to her then. "If you can tell me how to handle my lonely feelings I've got forever," she said.

"Well," I warned her, "neither of us has that kind of time right now, Marleen, and frankly, I don't think that we will need it. But I will tell you something that has helped me a lot in understanding what loneliness could or could not do for me. I think telling you about this now would be of more value to you than any advice I could think to give. I can tell you about me, and we'll see where that goes for you, O.K.?"

"O.K." she answered, and so I began. "I know something about looking into mirrors, Marleen, just as you do. Do you recall the first time we met and you spent the first hour we were together trying to prove to me that I could not help you with your lonely feelings? You couldn't help yourself either? And I said, 'Since you're here why not stick around awhile and find out if this is true. Who knows?'" And we talked up a storm, Marleen and I. I told her a lot about my own life, and I learned something about myself at the same time.

Even as I was telling her about myself, I was realizing quite clearly how I had, over the years, unknowingly magnified certain events in my mind. My earlier sense of loss and feelings at my own stupidity, feelings that had been so traumatic to me and shaped my life were thoughts to which I had been overly sensitive to the point of distortion. The feeling of deprivation, and the series of losses that I remembered suffering, were the self-imposed internalizations of a young man who simply did not know life's answers and *filled in the spaces anyway*. I feel this was true for Marleen also. It stunned me to realize how I had been affected by circumstances that were never as drastic as I had imagined. Recognizing this took away many excuses that I might have been tempted to use as an ongoing rationale for my subsequent behaviors or feelings.

Marleen and I felt like survivors. She felt that she had been damaged by her history of losing important people. The events that we had separately experienced were real, but the overimportance that we gave to them is what brought about the confusion. The misrepresentations that I, for one, had developed in my mind were crazy because there I was, a kid still feeling abandoned, when my adoptive parents were lovely people who just adored me. I knew that. And over the ten year period that I was sent away to different boarding schools, they hadn't done it to get rid of me. As a matter of fact they had done it at considerable financial sacrifice. They thought they were sending me to Florida for my health and then on to other boarding schools for the best education a kid could have.

Frankly, in a way, it saved my life. They tried me in the local grade school for three months and I couldn't function. I was a dismal failure and at that time, quite incapable of being a "student." So, in spite of Marleen's protestations, my feeling is that we shared some amazing similarities. I had allowed myself to remain insecure for too long. It wasn't until I got to college that I came to recognize that *enough is enough*. I had to stop myself by sheer willpower from the self-perpetuating nonsense that it was safer not to try than to try and fail.

I cannot recall when I first faced up to my tendency to see myself as intellectually inferior, but I think it came around the time that I worked nights behind the counter in the college drugstore. When I first began to work there I had trouble making proper change for a customer whenever someone was demanding or in a hurry. I first adapted to the anxiety about this by turning away from the customer when they handed me the money and facing towards the cash register where I could suddenly feel comfortable enough to get my mind unblocked, and make change easily.

I finally licked this phobia by determining not to turn away so quickly or simply close out my awareness of the customer's presence. My satisfaction in overcoming this problem was unbounded. I could visualize myself dropping away other inhibiting beliefs, and I managed to lose some, and it was so great I'll never forget it. These very small accomplishments may have seemed nothing to other people, but they were enormous to me. Success in trying became empowering. Even failing at something I was trying to do no longer held its overwhelming sting, for my intermittent successes stayed in my mind. In fact, I would look for positive things that I could begin to rebuild with from the experience of a failure. A ten thousand pound weight had been removed from my heart. I wanted to let everybody know that *faith is the beginning*.

But now, even as I had been telling these events to Marleen, I could sense her still finding it difficult to listen. Inside her the old doubting part of herself was saying over and over again, "yes, but that is not me, your experiences were not my experiences."

It has taken her a long time to admit that she has managed quite well considering the things with which she has had to deal. The inner core of that "lonely hell," as she describes it, will always be there in some degree. But she has emerged from her personal struggles to become a fine person, someone to be cherished, partially because of them.

The fact that I had been a lonely person no longer surprises me. If you asked me whether this was good or bad I would have to say "good," because I learned from it how damaging and unnecessary distrust in the self can be. At the same time, I have reaffirmed the promise I made to myself never to hide from feelings—good or bad, pleasurable or painful.

There have been some tough reminders along the way. The voice of Pat Hanson was one of these. It was not a friendly voice. She wanted the other members of the week-long training group for counselors that I was leading, to see who I really was. She needed most of all to hold the mirror to my face and make me see what she felt. Her words were bitter, invective.

"You rescuing, son-of-a-bitch," she screamed. "Hiding behind that God-damned beatific smile. You're like a God-damned nun! So helpful, so reaching out to help each of us deal with our garbage. And you sit there with your beautiful smile, and you hide from us. And, all the while we've talked about us. You sat there saying nothing about *Dick Price*."

I knew suddenly how right she had been. I had misunderstood my role as facilitator at this point in the group's development. This was not a "therapy group" and my personal involvement would not have taken away from the individual learning of the group members.

Pat leaned slowly forward into the circle, sitting cross-legged on a pillow, her tight-fisted knuckles pressing the floor. Finally, after what seemed in interminable silence, she straightened up and held both hands out towards me across the circle. Her words came now in a soft question.

"While you were helping me, you were hiding, weren't you?"

My mind flashed to the way I had supported her in dealing with the group's censure of her at our meeting the evening before. The words I was hearing now were not the words I would have liked to hear.

In truth, I had not meant to be deceiving, or holding back. The group had been rolling along quite well on its own I thought. The voice from my early training experience cautioned me now to turn her questions back to her to answer for herself. But another voice, seemingly truer at the moment, spoke just the opposite. "You are right," I said, as steadily as I could muster. "Right, in that I need to share more of myself with you, wrong, that I tried to hide. But you picked up on something that has troubled me over a good part of my life. The hidden me, the seed of which probably began in the very early years of my life." I did a lot of talking that night also, feeling that my sharing something about my own life with them was the most loving thing that I could do at that time.

That experience has stayed with me over the years. Certainly as time has passed I have examined again and again the ways I did or did not hold back from being honest in sharing with people. To me it seems to be a question of balance. My sharing with many groups seems to have helped them to share more equally with me.

I am reminded that a friend of mine, Lee Wotherspoon, has pointed out another aspect of this same topic. Lee has developed a set of guiding principles which people may review and use to evaluate the way that they manage their lives. His concern is with people who wish to increase their capacity for enjoyment and peak experiences. Lee's *principal of balance* seems particularly useful to people who are currently lonely:

"Balance is not a static unchanging state, but a rhythmic flow toward course correcting and rounding out! Emotional maturity and good mental health involve sensitively maintaining a flexible, flowing balance between needs and the pressures around us. It is what the ancient Greeks meant by the *Golden Mean—the secret of life is balance.*"

Stability, or balance, means not allowing ourselves to become too biased on one side of our feelings at the expense of the other side. An example might be that the acuteness of lonely feelings often exclude the realization that loneliness is seldom a condition which continues over a long period. Another principal might be seeing things always from the pessimistic side. Life does not present itself as only "good" or only "bad."

Our attention to correcting these imbalances will help bring us back to a more stable and realistic position. These are normal corrections to be made on our internal compasses. Recognizing the existence of good and bad aspects of events will help center us. Especially when things seem to be slipping out of our control.

The comforting expression,"I'm O.K.," is what I call the "hooker." Whenever I have felt that I was in a bad state, when problems have arisen and some pulling together is demanded, I can usually manage to remind myself that "I'm O.K.," "It's O.K." Once I can hook onto this keying-in phrase, I calm down. I am then more able to begin getting a handle on what is needed to solve the dilemma. One way or another nothing stays static. Reaffirming my okayness becomes an opening, comforting response with the *Principal of Balance.*

Recently, I had a first-hand and somewhat lighthearted experience with this business of balancing both sides of a problem. A man who works as a mechanic in the local garage met me on the street one day and we got to talking. He was telling me about his divorce two years past and how lonely and depressed he still felt. When I asked him how he handles things he said that he was feeling so low that he couldn't find any way of reconnecting with anything right now. "When I went to the well it was dry," he said, with considerable finality.

I did not mean to be flip with a man in such obvious distress, but since we were standing outside of a small restaurant and it was close to noontime, I suggested we begin to fill up this well with drink, some food, and some good talk.

That was the time I told him one of my best kept secrets. I've noticed over the years that when I've needed to do some clear thinking, I tend to get good ideas in the bathtub rather than from the well. After a while our talking together seemed to be reenergizing him a little. I got around to telling him what I hoped would be an amusing, but useful experiment. "This is what you call a lighthearted way of dealing with heavyheartedness," I told him. "The next time you get into the bathtub (or take a walk, or find a quiet relaxing place), give yourself this simple three minute test. Let your mind "flow," metaphorically speaking. Allow your mind to seek new ideas. Clear away cobwebs. Shake off all the heavy dullness that has been weighing you down. "Over a three minute period you are to imagine that you are to become advisor to your best friend, or yourself, or both. Quickly, and in a kind of free-flow scattershot of ideas, you are going to throw out at least twenty different and original ideas for things that your friend could do right away to begin lifting his or her mood. It doesn't matter how crazy they are. You are not trying to evaluate." "Well," he said quizzically, "I'll try it. But I want you to do it with me."

We asked for two pieces of paper from the waiter, looked at our wrist watches and wrote down whatever ideas flashed to us. Together, getting into the spirit of the game, we generated a list that approximates this one:

1. Do something. Anything. Do it with people. Be a legend in your own time.
2. Get some balloons and tie them to your neighbor's mailbox.
3. If you won't tie it around your waist, at least tie it around your mind.
4. You like music—take some kind of lessons.

5. Visit your mother in the nursing home.

6. List five nice things about your ex-wife.

7. Start on your diet today. We estimate seven pounds would do it.

8. Call that person you've been too nervous to contact.

9. Change the oil in your car.

10. Write the President a letter.

11. Institute a "National Unloneliness Day" in your neighborhood. Everyone is to come out of their houses and shake hands with their neighbors, hug them, invite them in for breakfast, or to the nearest bar, soda fountain or tea house. After that? Optional.

12. When was the last time you took flowers to the people at the post office or bank? Try "Flower power."

13. Stand by the T.V. dinner section of the supermarket and you'll find people hungry to meet people. Ask which dinner tastes best, talk.

14. Take up walking, biking, or running regularly. We guarantee you will, over a two year period, find several silver spoons, knives, combs, money (five dollar bills, assorted change), plus other unmentionable articles. Other treasures with which you can:

15. Start a hope chest.

16. Ask someone you hardly know to go fishing with you.

17. Read a box of letters that you haven't read in years.

18. Tell someone they are nice.

19. Go to the singles group meeting at your church or any other church this week.

20. Let your spontaneous child emerge. Become the "nice" neighborhood eccentric. Learn to play!

21. Go dancing, roller skating, or

22. Try your radio. Music to waltz by. Boogaloo.

23. McDonald's is looking for "counter help - male."
"*STOP THE TIMER.*"

This was an example of spontaneous instant research. Not very scholarly, but fun. Try yours.

Do you know which one of the items on the list my friend, the mechanic chose? None of the above. He did say, however, that it sure was a pepper-upper! As we were leaving the restaurant he turned to me and said, "Actually, Dick, I don't think anything came out of this." Then he added, almost as an afterthought, "One thing I'm thinking right now, though, there was this great bumper sticker I saw the other day. Do you know what it said? It said, 'ALL THOSE WOMEN—SO LITTLE TIME!' Tonight I think I'm going to the Parents Without Partners meeting that I said I wouldn't touch with a ten-foot pole." (I ended up paying for the luncheon.)

★ ★ ★

Loneliness attacks people in all walks of life, some are rich, some poor, some intelligent, some limited.

Bob Walters is a most articulate man. One day I said to him, "People distrust themselves so much. They think loneliness is frightening. It's a shame. We know people are looking for answers. You have looked for answers to your own loneliness. They fear they will not be able to find their dreams. They don't recognize the power they have. Maybe you and I might try to give them some real examples of what someone *can* do."

"Bob, I want to try something with you for a moment. Let's assume that you and I are sitting here surrounded by dozens of these people. They are saying, 'How do we learn to handle our loneliness?' You are going to tell this group of people your own significant understandings of loneliness. What will you say to them? How will you start?"

"Well," he began, "I would begin by saying that there are many kinds of loneliness caused by many different factors, but that my own experiences are the only ones I can be sure of, I would say that people create their own loneliness as opposed to having it thrust upon them by others. My feeling is that if you reach out, you will find that "seek and you shall find" is true with respect to loneliness. But often people are incapable of reaching. And if they do reach, they usually more or less deliberately fumble the ball. I would say that basically you're alone because you're afraid of not being alone. Being alone hurts. But then, not being alone means commitment and that can cause disillusionment which hurts more. You can never have a secure love. It hurts to be in love and the thing you love might disappear tomorrow. And you know that, you can't help but know. The person or thing you love might reject you tomorrow. And if you know anything of the world, you know that these things happen every day. So basically, to extend your love might seem to be inherently frightening.

"Probably one of the most valuable effects of companionship is that it strengthens people who have a satisfying relationship. It gives you the strength to solve problems that otherwise you wouldn't be able to handle. It gives you the confidence to enjoy levels of happiness and pleasure that would otherwise be frightening. I have heard hundreds and hundreds of people say 'I can't believe it! It's too good to be true!' They can't believe it will last, and there are all kinds of comments like, 'How come I deserve this?' or 'How come I could possibly get this?' or 'It's a trick.' or 'Somebody is conning me,' or 'He or she is just setting me up for a fall.'

"It requires courage to be part of something or someone and to make them a part of you. And I think that for most people the greatest enemy they have is fear. Because the penalities of love are commensurate with the rewards. And while there is no relationship more rewarding than love, its loss can bring intense hurt. When you love someone, you're going to discover that, in addition to the ever-present threat that you may or may not be appreciated, or you may lose your love; there are going to be shared agonies as well as joy whoever it is you love. You have to accept the fact that there will be uncertainty and fear in your life. And there will always be pain—either the negative pain of loneliness which is very real, or what I'm talking about, because all of us have felt it in some degree or another at some time in our lives, or you take the uncertainty and sharing the problems that goes along with sharing peoples' lives.

"But more than anything else, I would just tell you to face your fear; seek, find, and overcome it. It's there, I know it's there. I mean, if you're human it has to be there. And if you say it's not there, you're hiding it from yourself."

"But," I asked Bob, "What if I'm not as strong as you think I am? What if you're giving me too much credit for being able to pull myself out of this."

"I'm not. It's perfectly true that most people can't sit down and write "I will be brave" one hundred times and then have the courage of a lion. But what you can do is to discover situations that more or less demand that you behave in courageous ways. Force yourself to act in prescribed ways and you will discover that in performing these actions you were really not as afraid as you thought you were. *Courage is the ability to proceed, even though you are fearful.* And practically everybody can do this to some extent. Finding out how much you can do is difficult, painful. But it's the one thing that can put your mind at ease, because after you face the trial of behaving as if you were brave, you will discover that all the things that you have not been doing because you didn't think you were brave enough to do them, are possible. In other words, you can only discover you have courage by surviving the situations that demand it. Therefore, I'm telling you not to fear being afraid because you can perform courageously although you are fearful and learn how to live. And once you have faced the danger and survived it, you will then be more able and more willing to face other dangers.

"Basically, life is a progression of frights. You go from one frightening experience that you survive and when that becomes a thing you can endure and do again to new levels of experiences, and as you prevail over the new ordeal, and you discover that, 'Yeah, it's scary and very painful, but I can do it.' And if you're looking for an analogy, think back to when you first were learning to ride a bike. You knew other people knew how to do it because you saw them do it every day. Every kid was doing it, and you wanted to do it too. But those wheels really wobbled and it moved fast, and if you fell down you might get hurt. But eventually, you know the combination of desire, pride, peer group pressure, what have you, they got you on the bike. Perhaps you were terrified, and you wobbled around, but you kept going.

"Maybe you even fell off a couple of times and got hurt, but you got right back up and tried again. And in the back of your mind there's always the knowledge that riding a bicycle is dangerous. But nonetheless, having faced your fear and defeated it, riding a bike became a commonplace, ordinary, normal, and routine part of your life."

Now I would like to share a different type of challenge and a different view of how you can draw from your own inner strength, and overcome fear. I use these examples to re-emphasize the benefits of making the move away from *yearning* to act to *direct action* leading to *involvement*, and on to real *change*. Let me take you back to a previous incident that took place in one of the first poetry groups I participated in as leader.

All members of the group were to write about something personally important to us. The writing was to act as a kind of catharsis in that we would hope to better understand the emotional parts of the related experience after we had expressed it on paper. We had agreed not to hold back our feelings in writing this poem, and also not to use the tired old excuse that we "didn't know how." This group had been designed as a poetry group for people who were sure that they could not write poetry—for people who knew they couldn't and who wouldn't dare read their own poetry, even if they could—"Closet poets" who lock the door.

A middle-aged woman joined us a few weeks after we had begun the group at the local library. We encouraged her not to worry that she hadn't brought anything to read. "Just be with us," we said, "and maybe someday you will either find a poem that strikes you and you will bring it in and read it to us, or you might even write one yourself. "Oh, no, no, no, I couldn't do that," she said. "No way. But I am enjoying being with you, and I hope it is all right. I'm a little embarrassed that I'm not offering anything."

Then two or three weeks later she came in one evening and sat along the side of the wall. She had been sitting quietly throughout the hour and half session, and it was getting near wind-up time. She began to fumble with something deep in her pocketbook, and she brought out a tiny crumpled paper. I swear it must have been torn off the corner of a phone book page. Slowly she unfolded it, and said, "You know, I did write something. But it's not really poetry." And I said to her, "Well, we didn't tell you to, but we said if you wanted to, you could. And so why don't you share it with us."

With shaking hands she held up the paper. It was a tense, but fascinating moment. She cleared her throat, apologized once again for the "non-poetry" she said she had produced, got out her glasses and adjusted them on her face, looked hopelessly around the room and said in a scared whisper, "I can't read it myself. Somebody else read it. I can't do it."

And I said, "You are the author; you would read it with your own perspective; we couldn't do that nearly as well as you. Please read it to us," and she did! She took a chance and came out into the light. Here is what she wrote:

"There are lillies in my backyard.
They please me very much
Like this group."

That was a beginning for her, and for us, too, because she turned out to be a fine poet.

It is spellbinding, really, to see someone begin to find things outside their demoralized selves and get hooked on something that energizes them, and connects them to their own natural creativeness. We all dream of things we want to do but rarely risk starting to do them, which is the surest way out of boredom and depression. Sometimes it takes people a long and agonized time to risk even the most simple way of expressing their own creativity. Dreams, like words, are impotent until something becomes generated because of them. In attempting to reach out toward our own visions, we stretch our minds and our wills. By not lying down and giving up, we open our eyes to possibility. Some people live with blinders on. They cannot take time to see beauty, time hangs heavy on them, yet new experiences can be only moments away.

If you can, for example, allow yourself to experience sunshine in all its graduation of color and mood, feel the essence of the day, appreciate it, you are so fortunate, because there are people who do not. Locked away inside themselves, these people look at daylight blindly. It has no feeling of grandeur or warmth for them. They look at blue sky and feel the grayness in their hearts.

Their tragedy is one of shutting themselves inside themselves in disillusioned self-absorptions and distrust. I feel we have to ask what lessons can be learned from this? How to move towards trusting oneself? For one thing, we can begin to accept our part in being the way we are—whatever we have been, done, failed at, cheated at, and not hide from it. It is a time to reach inside for truth and discover the strength that is there.

Sometimes help comes from the most unexpected resources. That tiny key that bolsters us. It might be simply the words to a song we hear on our daily travels, or a phrase, a quotation, or story which inspires and strengthens us. One of these is a quotation that hangs on the wall of a small clinic where I practiced for a number of years. It is a cherished reminder to me:

DESIDERATA
Go placidly amid the noise & haste, & remember
what peace there may be in silence. As far as possible

without surrender be on good terms with all persons. Speak your truth quietly & clearly; and listen to others, even the dull & ignorant; they too have their story. Avoid loud & aggressive persons, they are vexations to the spirit. If you compare yourself with others, you may become vain & bitter; for always there will be greater & lesser persons than yourself. Enjoy your achievements as well as your plans. Keep interested in your own career, however humble; it is a real possession in the changing fortunes of time. Exercise caution in your business affairs; for the world is full of trickery. But let this not blind you to what virtue there is; many persons strive for high ideals; and everywhere life is full of heroism. Be yourself. Especially, do not feign affection. Neither be cynical about love; for in the face of all aridity & disenchantment it is perennial as the grass. Take kindly the counsel of the years, gracefully surrendering the things of youth. Nurture strength of spirit to shield you in sudden misfortune. But do not distress yourself with imaginings. Many fears are born of fatigue & loneliness. Beyond a wholesome discipline, be gentle with yourself. You are a child of the universe, no less than the trees & the stars; you have a right to be here. And whether or not it is clear to you, no doubt the universe is unfolding as it should. Therefore be at peace with God, whatever you conceive Him to be, and whatever your labors & aspirations, in the noisy confusion of life keep peace with your soul. With all its sham, drudgery & broken dreams, it is still a beautiful world. Be careful. Strive to be happy.

A former mentor of mine, and a friend, agreed to share with me, and with you, the story of a turning point in his own torturous climb out of despondency and fear. It is a message that touches us. It demonstrates again the essential power of the will that each of us can draw from within ourselves:

"I used to feel alone and kind of separate from everybody. Those were terrible feelings. . . . They were very poignant and painful, and it was only much later that I could capitalize on them and try to see the constructive part of them. I learned to use this to reassess my own uniqueness and my capacity to stand outside and be separate from any situation which has the emotional impact of loneliness. I experienced a degree of potency in allowing myself to see the situation I was in as though from the outside. That became one of the most defensive, and yet constructive ways to which I used to put my loneliness.

"In large part now, I believe, the loneliness became the fulcrum around which I became a businessman as well as a member of the "helping" profession, observing people, observing myself, and in that way using it for constructive purposes. In addition, I used it in the sense of emphasizing my being different. Previously being different was painful, and I didn't want to be different. Again, out of maturity and growing awareness of myself, I could then turn it around and see where it led. It's more valuable to be different than to be similar or common, because the common wasn't all that great. I see that it's possible at this retrospective time to recognize that a lot of the force and power that came into making me what I was, came out of this awareness.

"So, although I didn't know it at the time, it sort of led into my philosophy that I could always convert a negative into a positive. At first, I didn't believe in that philosophy, yet, as I grow older that is the sort of a principle I use in my life, that 'Yes, this is terrible. Now how can I convert it into something constructive. . . .' Either you're going to do it now or you are never going to do it. It's again that desperate state, but you know you don't have that much more life to go, and so if you are going to continue with those old patterns, you can go on with your depression and your self-indulgence. I can go on feeling sorry for myself and saying 'Oh, my God, you know, I've got a raw deal in this whole business of having lost my father,' but, you know, that doesn't make sense any-more. You can only do that for so long, and you can go on for the rest of your life, or you can change it. And I decided I was going to change it, and it was really very interesting. It was surprising!

"Having had particularly extensive self-analysis (psychoanalysis) my orientation had been, 'Well, if you're depressed you have to analyze it more clearly. It's not a matter of willpower.' But then finally one day I said, 'Look I'm not going to be depressed any-more. It's really absurd, and it is going to be an act of working through. You can't just work through some issues on account of your father's early death at an age when you were very vulnerable. You've just got to live with that as an experience that you had which had devastating effects and which gets minimized or modified a lot.' But my feeling was that I had com-mitted myself an indulgence in being lonely and de-pressed. It's giving yourself over to self-pity. And even though I don't want to sound moralistic or harsh about it. I said in a very detached way, that 'I wasn't going to do that anymore or even permit it from hap-pening again, and I stopped being lonely and de-pressed just like that.' It was an act of will.

"I did keep working on the issue of my father's death. I knew that was the key. It was quite obvious to me. The key was also that I had been using that as a shield, you see, and that I was also using it as an excuse. That's against my own insight. You can go waving that about. 'I have the right to be depressed because my father died at an early age,' and then you've got it all locked in. There's no need—You've got an excuse—justifiable, understandable psycho-logically sound. *You don't change.*

"To me, loneliness and depression are the same thing. When I'm not lonely, I'm not depressed. It's as simple as that."

★ ★ ★

Quite possibly no one would believe it, but it if were in some way possible to produce a book about Loneliness containing only one paragraph on a single page, between two covers, I would hope to see it feature the importance of WILL (power).

We have to stop blaming ourselves for things over which we have no control. Life is not always predictable. However, we can make a dramatic alteration in our Life-Style. Changes that will strongly effect the positive outcome in our insecure and lonely feelings. Contrary to some cultural beliefs, we can do this instantly, if the WILL is there.

TEN

NOT TO SAY: "GOODBYE" UNTIL YOU SAY "HELLO" (Aging and the Therapeutic Life-Style)

> We search for something that will seem like truth to us; we search for understanding; we search for that principal which keys us deeply into the pattern of all life; we search for the relation of things, one to the other.
>
> T. S. Eliot

I stopped my car at a green traffic light to watch a long funeral procession of passing cars, headlights on. I remembered at that moment a childrens' poem that my mother recited to me after our next door neighbor had passed away, and I was asking what death was all about:

> *Deep in my heart*
> *I thought with pride*
> *I know someone*
> *Who has died.*

I thought, too, of the statement attributed to Woody

Allen, who said that he was not so much afraid of dying as he just didn't want to be there when it happened.

But someone close by had died, as this cortege proved. Leading the line of over thirty cars was the typical black Cadillac hearse, closely followed by two other Cadillacs carrying members of the family.

All those people, I thought, paying last respects to one human being. In my mind's eye I joined with them in that slow caravan to the ready earth of the gravesite. I wondered what special eulogy would be spoken over this departed? Or over any one of us for that matter, should we be there?

That we had lived a "good life?" That we had been a gentle person? Or that the way we had lived exemplified the highest spiritual values? And, what about our accomplishments? Would a count of the number of people or cars in our funeral procession have any measurable relationship to the degree of respect we had enjoyed while alive? Such a point scoring seems to me an act of futility. What matters in assessing the worth of a human life is something quite different.

You and I are currently in a position to do a lot of living. We are at the opportune position between past and future that allows us chance for reflection. Since we cannot go back, the future belongs to us. In that thoughtful place I want to look at what my life means and how I live it, I am often reminded of a composite of borrowed words that helps me view with new insight how to get involved in living the kind of life that is most rewarding to me. It goes like this:

"LETTERS NEVER WRITTEN—PROMISES TO KEEP"

And, I think, there is so much that I want to do that is unfinished. Aging, which began for each one of us at the moment of conception, moves irrovacably toward us and opens again these private but inevitable questions:

— Where have I been?

— Where am I now?

— Where am I going?

Only we can fill in the blanks. How we go about this will determine how we see ourselves, as well as how other people will know us. "Oh, but it is too late to change my life now," some might say. Or, "Is this all there is?" "What else is there for me?" Such conjectures are sad, really, because anyone who will look even quickly around them will see that even one additional minute of life affords possibilities for change.

Of course we haven't fulfilled our life expectations—-there is always something to look forward to—something important we have not yet done that can be accomplished with the rest of our years. For example, if your kids, your wife, or that "special person" in your life does not love you right now, you have urgent reasons to see the years ahead as an opportunity to make corrections. Perhaps it will mean shifting the center of your focus back to their needs, as well as your own. Time is a chance to reclaim or revise your birthright option. Make the remainder of your life what you think it should be. Look into a mirror, see yourself.

I don't believe that looking towards what we still hope to accomplish is so very difficult. You see, I can't help thinking that all of us are looking for much the same things. We may talk about our wants differently, or accent one more than the other, but I am saying that we each share simple common hopes for ourselves. First of all to feel emotionally and physically connected to something. To believe that our lives have value and meaning, and to experience our daily living as the pleasurable, creative extension of ourselves. And naturally, Love is an integral part of all this. In all likelihood we also share one other important desire, to leave something of ourselves behind—to be remembered.

A friend of mine, an accountant who lives down the street, was telling me how shocked he was the other day to arrive at work and hear that one of his colleagues had died three or four days before. He had not heard about it until his boss came into the office saying, "Too bad about Jim, wasn't it?'' It really jolted him, because his boss had just come back from the man's funeral feeling he had represented the company and had not gone out of his way to tell other employees who might also have gone.

It made my friend feel that each person in this company was really insignificant and it brought to the surface feelings of his own essential aloneness. He expressed it as seeing himself as the pebble dropped into a pond of quiet water. Very shortly after the pebble first rippled the surface, the water became still and quiet again as though he, the pebble, had never existed.

At the same time it led him to think about how he was treating the woman with whom he now lived. He knew, regrettably, that he had acted distant and not been as involved with her as she would have liked. He told me this with great difficulty, his face ashen, and he said he now realized how shallow his relationships were, and he wanted to run back to those people while he still could and say how much he had needed and appreciated them.

He was recognizing as we talked that there were many unsaid words inside of him, words he had never spoken to the people who were important to him. Just simple things like "I love you," or "You are important to me." He saw ahead of him a chance to make amends, to change. One of these modifications would be to continue to do his job as well as he could, but not keep putting in so many "late night" hours. He would spend much, much more time working at his personal life.

I felt as though he had partially realized most of these things for some time but had been galvanized into awareness by the unexpected announcement of his colleague's death. The conversation was obviously an important one for both of us, so we walked across the road to a small park and kept on talking.

We agreed that when we were younger we had each placed much importance on material needs, such as a "sharp" looking car, a nice apartment, etc. We had apparently used these possessions as metaphors to express a part of ourselves as we wanted to be seen. Neither of us liked having placed such emphasis on possessions, and over the years had almost over-reacted by trying to de-emphasize such things. One of the first steps I had taken was to sell the little Porsche that I had fixed up and cherished for seven years. He had stopped trying to make his house the "show-place" of the neighborhood.

We found ourselves comparing notes on how each of us had tried to achieve a balance between what we really needed and what we owned for pleasure. Coming from two entirely different backgrounds and perspectives, we both had found that it was important to have shucked the need to "look good" in the old materialistic ways.

I can remember what a relief it was for me to recognize that power and status had little real value compared to the things I really aspired to. And I began at that time to notice and appreciate more and more those friends I had who were not consumed with possessions so much as they were by the quality of their being with the people they cared about.

I knew that this was one of the strongest driving forces in my own life. I needed to continue to be more involved in my own family life, with my kids, with my wife, with our relatives, as well as with many other people who were very important to me. It would take further effort on my part to balance this personal dimension of my life with my own love of my work, and my other creative activities. I recognized that I had not always achieved this balance in the past but was comforted by the fact that as long as we are alive there is time for restitution.

I think of a young fellow I know who feels himself a failure. He and his dad are sadly isolated from each other. Each one is sure that if only the other would shape up, things between them would improve. The father is saying to himself, "How could he be such a twerp! So ungrateful for all that we have tried to do." And the kid is saying, "Asshole father, what the hell does he expect from me?" Both of them are hungry for a relationship with each other.

Dad wants to be proud of his son. Son wants him to be proud, but there is a catch, neither will make that first gesture necessary if they are to know one another better.

They are both hurt, and the way they have adapted to this is through anger. But anger alone only sets them further apart and somehow they have to get in touch with their inner feelings of disappointment in their separate life's dream. If they are both looking for love, not hate, one of them will have to mobilize, to make a move out of this damaging position. They cannot change each other, they can only change themselves. The son, for example, might just throw up his hands in frustration and say, "Hey, Pop, let's try liking each other for a change! Dinner is on me, and we are going to talk this thing out." Or, the father could say to himself, or his son,"Look, he is my son. He is a lot like me unfortunately and we may never completely relate to each other, but we are 'family' and I want to love him." And so it might go, each person making his own moves to fulfill his dreams—to feel connected. But someone has to start that movement toward affiliation.

If each understood the pressure of time, how the specter of loneliness continually challenges us with choices between *love* and *fear*, perhaps they would resolve their differences before it is too late. The paradox, as I see it, is that love is only authentic when we are not afraid to share it with someone else and yet part of love is fear.

The reality of aging brings with it the presence of "beginnings" as well as "endings." Both become more precious because of the ebbing of time. We can see that whatever we are going to do we had best get on with it. But how we transit from the intellectual "here" to the actual "there" is what counts.

I thought about this during a recent work/vacation trip to Sarasota, Florida. Following my habit of getting up around six-thirty I put on my bathing trunks and took a long walk along the tide-line of the Gulf beach. It struck me that of the dozen or so early beach walkers that I passed

close by, only about half of them acknowledged our passing with a "good morning" or a nod. My sense was that we
were a small unique group of people who enjoyed this
sunrise experience and so we shared something in common yet few of us acknowledged our relationship.

As the morning passed and I walked along, other people
began joining us and I became fairly adept at determining
beforehand who would, and who would not, offer some
greeting. Many of the passers-by looked towards me as we
met, but their eyes slid downward and away as we approached. Others looked straight ahead, oblivious. A few
were obviously involved in their own reverie or looking for
sea shells as they walked. I found it interesting that almost
consistently the faster walkers and/or the people who carried themselves most erect, were the ones I could count on
to say "hello," or to nod.

I was quite engrossed in these observations as I walked
back towards the small beach apartments that I had left,
when I noticed a woman waving to me from the porch. I
turned and walked over to where she sat on the porch steps
munching on a breakfast roll. "Hi," I said, as I approached
her, thinking that she might have mistaken me for someone she knew. "Good morning," she answered smiling. "I
saw you yesterday morning about this same time and I
noticed how you seemed to be enjoying yourself. So today,
when I saw you striding along, I just wanted to wave to
you."

"That makes me feel nice that you would do that," I
exclaimed. I told her about my little impromptu experiment in communications and how good it was finishing
my walk with such an outgoing greeting from her. We had
a great talk and finally she told me that she and her husband had to leave this very morning to go home to Indiana.
This important meeting would be a "highlight of her day."
"Me too," I assured her. Often memorable exchanges
which begin spontaneously whether they occur between
strangers or friends have profound meanings.

I can understand peoples' natural hesitation at times

when they sense that being too forward is inappropriate, but I feel that we often hold back too much and so remain strangers when that is the very least thing we want for ourselves. You might just want to pay attention sometimes to whether you, almost without knowing it, avoid engagement with other people that you might meet this way by dropping your eyes or some other method of avoidance. Daily life is generally one of routine and activities that bring us in constant contact with other people. If we look at ourselves and don't like how our relationships are going we may have to bite the bullet, make some shifts in our way of being with others. For some it will mean PROMISES KEPT - LETTERS WRITTEN.

There are, or will be, times when problems are not of our own making. We become innocently caught in having to adapt to situations which either we could not have anticipated, or which were going to happen without our say-so. But even here, we are compelled to choose between finding a replacement solution or remaining disengaged and possibly feeling a victim of whatever happens.

Over the years I have found it useful to put my thoughts down on paper when I am trying to work out a sense of direction. I enjoy using this journal approach, and for certain periods of time I might keep a journal of ideas and experiences that I am involved in. Putting thoughts down on paper helps me understand and simplify, I hope, whatever thoughts and feelings I am experiencing.

In the more reflective atmosphere of aging there seems to be more time for ongoing consolidation of things felt and observed. I suppose it is much the same thing that artists experiences as they mature in expressing through their special media those ideas that have meaning for them.

A friend of mine has used writing, both to herself and to God, as one way of attempting to look to her own future. She is currently in a lot of pain. She tries to work it through by dialoguing her feelings to God and interprets his answers to her.

"Judith, listen. Don't be afraid. This is a growing stage for you. Do not run from all the feelings that you feel. I know the love you have for him. I love him too. He is moving on to another stage of his growth. It is not easy for him to move away from people he has been with.

The pain you are feeling is great. But, the strength and growth that you are going to find as a person is going to be worth it. Don't close off. Don't shut your feelings off.

Only you can be in control of this. You can go back to not trusting and shrivel up and die emotionally, or you can face it, and walk through it. Which do you choose?"

"I choose growth, but I am afraid that I cannot make it without him."

"Judith, you have grown slowly, but you will find a willingness inside of you to grow more. Growing and standing on your own two feet is going to be a learning experience. I am with you. You have people around you to help support you, but that is all it is going to be, support, not dependency."

In her anguish, Judith can barely manage to see within herself a source of strength in the days, months, and years ahead. But she realizes this becomes another time of choice between love and fear, (fear expressed in withdrawal). Of denying the value of the person who must leave, or accepting that if the relationship had any meaning at all she will retain within her the best that person could give.

The fear is often that we will not find someone else who will love us. So often that fear is unfounded. In the end we all have to take responsibility for our behavior as well as our attitude. I guess we are always relearning this, aren't we? That is what continually intrigues us, to discover more about ourselves.

And quite possibly, for reasons which you may not even have been aware of at the time, it was this very need that led you to walk into a bookstore somewhere and come away with this particular book. But the book is not what is important. You are. You started this process on your own, so it must have relevance. No one, including myself, has felt lonely or depressed and not tried to do something about it without first experiencing a sense of loss of:

— Love
— Self-Esteem
— Control

When I first began to develop what I now refer to as the THERAPEUTIC LIFE-STYLE I did not fully understand how paramount these issues would become. I do now because I have seen how miserable life can be when a sense of completeness or balance is missing. The fat lady wants to be thin. The thin man wants to be more robust. The weak person wants to be stronger. The sad person wants more laughter. The lonely person longs to feel connection. It does not matter what degree of imbalance you are experiencing. It might only be the vague feelings that you are not sure what's wrong with the way you are living, but you know something doesn't feel right.

So I think of three factors, love, self-esteem, and control of one's life, as super important to each of us. It helps me to view them separately, but also as part and parcel of a reinforcing triangle which is connected in much the same way that our *mind, body* and *behaviors* are:

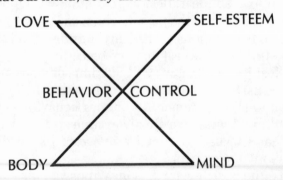

To me, our bodies and our minds are the substructures which each of us was born with, and are therefore the vehicles through which all else becomes possible. It seems a personal tragedy when people disrespect either of these aspects of themselves through laziness, abuse, or lack of appreciation, for how profoundly beautiful they are.

As I look at this visual design I can see how the parts interconnect. You and I cannot, for example, experience love without first recognizing how much a part of love our mind plays. And still, our body and mind each feels different aspects of Love. There would be no expression of Love without behavior, and so on. Each enriches the other.

I keep thinking how we do have time available to make it a better life. time is represented in the hourglass shape formed by these six necessary elements. They are a constant reminder to me to try and keep *my view of life in the most simple but clear terms*—and not muddy up the waters by throwing in self-doubt and recrimination. Achieving these goals is the heart of the therapeutic Life-Style as I envision it. It is simply taking the important separate aspects of life and working to improve them in the same emotional and physically healthy way that an athlete might train.

It means constant attention to doing things more gracefully, developing our sense of mastery, trying out skills, building up physical as well as emotional stamina. This is seen as a long-term improvement plan to achieve the highest degree of wellness possible. The athlete usually finds that with attention and determination more can be done than first expected. I believe this is true of developing ourselves as well as of performing well.

Characteristically, I tend to reduce important issues to fit within some simple principles that I can both make sense of and use. This need to simplify comes from a strong belief that we often make things too hard for ourselves and thus cannot move forward. No mystery, no excuses. If we search out our own philosophical essentials—attempt to follow our dreams, being the best we can possibly be, finding love, and feeling well, we can live up to our finest potential being, develop our own unique solutions to living fully.

This is why I have tried to develop a therapeutic Life-Style that will hopefully improve the lonely aspects of life. There are some advantages in our advancing age. We have been through many experiences already so we can benefit from earlier mistakes. This gets us back in the driver's seat. Once there, I believe, it behooves us to appreciate that the first step is to convince ourselves that there is a second step. For me, one way to do this is to continue plumping up my Life-Style with a few well-meaning admonitions, quieting reminders that I am "O.K." and *I am to fully enjoy the remainder of the time I have available.* Some of the encouragements that I particularly like to keep before me are these:

1. Go gentle — In that I see the target ahead as something I will gradually get closer to. Make peace with myself, and above all, don't put roadblocks in the way.
2. Appreciate Time — Everything takes on new meaning as I allow myself room to do things at a pace I can control. Non-distracting time alone can become peaceful and gratifying.
3. Stay away from answers — When I find answers I have locked the door to growth. The fun is in the unfolding chase of truth.
4. Pursue play seriously — Sprinkle with humor.
5. Accept struggle with gratitude. For without struggle there can be no success.

"Success" is an inspiring word. So is "happiness," but they seem elusive concepts when you are trying to discover their location when they are missing from your life. The word "wellness" is much more easily obtained because it implies a condition that you can attain, and yet it often leads to the other conditions you seek.

Wellness means emotional as well as physical health. One aspect of this would be that for us to feel very well we should make every effort to attain the best condition we can in all areas of our life. Adapting successfully to adversity is a part of reinforcing our wellness.

A story, I believe, about this healthfulness occurred the other day as I sat at my desk to do some writing. My head was full of ideas. But I was stopped short in my tracks. I could not write, even though I knew I had things that I wanted to say. It was an experience that I had been through at other times in my life. I said to myself, "What am I doing, writing this book?" I know quite a lot about the intricacies of loneliness, and I understand a good bit about how people deal with it. But my goal is not to *tell* anyone about themselves. My goal is to help them *find their own answers.*

So as I sat there on that particular Sunday reflecting, knowing that it would be valuable to shut down my "producing" element and dwell in a quiet, listening frame of mind.

I noticed outside the window that a slight wind was blowing. I listened to my breathing. As I sat there I became quite and peaceful within myself. And what came to me then, without my active volition intruding, were answers to questions, answers I had subconsciously known, but were located beyond my conscious mind. They needed a period of meditation to renew things that I had felt today and yesterday, and the day before that. They came to me because they had always been there, and suddenly I became able to hear them.

I grew up in a world full of other people's answers. My parents and those around me gave advice on how life was, the world was, and how I might live in it. I listened peripherially as the young often do. They rarely spoke of loneliness, or aging, or death in any significant detail.

They did help me to see that even those close to us are fallible. That *their* answers to life were *their answers* to life, that in many ways there are no final "givens" to the most important questions, that is where faith begins—an answer to no answers.

My experience of my parents, and those important other people, taught me something valuable. I would have to seek my own explanations as a child of the universe of wind, rain, sun, shadow, air, fire and of earth. And I saw that there were no answers beyond my own interpretation of these phenomena of experience. I learned that my whole life task was simply to begin taking responsibility for the way that I would live, and finally for the way I would die.

There was something enormously comforting in this reviewing concept of my life's meaning. Through my own inner re-vision I saw that I had only one choice, and it seemed an attractive and reassuring one—to recognize without compromise, how my actions, my feelings, thoughts, spirituality are ME. This is the beginning, the middle and the end of who I am—or who I can be. My philosophic therapeutic-oriented life-style is just one person's way of managing. As I look back upon the short reflective experience I enjoyed that Sunday, I think again how important an ingredient of "Wellness" is being able to maintain a balanced sense of humor. When I told my wife, Jean, about this experience she said, "Well, did you expect a revelation? Aren't we always rediscovering universal truth?"

And then she reminded me of a lovely present she had given me on my birthday some years before. It was a pewter figurine of a small barefoot boy balancing along a railroad track holding something in his uplifted hand which we can't quite identify. There is a nice sense of boyish exuberance in this figure, as well as what Jean calls "irrepressibility." One of the better things that we might hope people would say in remembrance of us would be that we were "irrepressible." That they saw in us a quality of resiliency that allowed us to bounce back and pick up again when things were difficult.

I can remember many times in my life when I made some vow to improve on something I was, or was not doing. Whether it was to be a better person, lover, father, friend, or whatever. I determined, at diferent points, to change things for the better. A lot of my resolutions probably just bounced off the walls and went nowhere, but some of them stuck. Usually, if I can envision myself realistically doing whatever is desired over a sustained period of time, I have a better chance of success. I realize that the only way I can change the habit of thinking about doing valuable things and then not doing them, is to remind myself how good I will feel when I make a solid beginning and then follow through.

There is a broad latitude to what will maintain our feelings of success and happiness within the wellness spectrum. Consider another viewpoint:

"Master, What is Wellness?"
"Sir, Wellness is living successfully."
"Master, tell me how did you learn these things?"
"Sir, by living unsuccessfully, and feeling lousy."

It Is Not Loneliness That Should Concern Us

At this point if we go back to the theme of loneliness now we will find that a new pattern has been emerging. We no longer need to be concerned with searching for a strategy for avoiding Loneliness per se. *What is needed instead is our own system for living as fully as we can, and in the most satisfactory manner.*

I believe that whatever your present physical and mental capacities, whatever your age or your circumstances, you can, in some small way, envision and create something better. I believe you are capable of beginning to look at specific ways to improve. These do not have to be dramatic or spectacular but I think they could enrich your future if you will only imagine them into being.

If we just let the smallest glimmer of hope into our daily lives we begin to feel in control again, and increase our self-esteem in the process. This "good energy" they inspire brings renewed vigor. This may free us to find greater fulfillment in our own private lives which would include loving others.

Have you heard the saying, "If you need something done

ask the busy person?" The busy person, being engaged in doing something significant is energized and finds more time to be helpful. Such words as "perfection," being the "best you can," etc., may seem trite, or typical TV sports-announcer jargon to your ear. At the moment your life may appear to you to be a dull "nothing-will-ever-change" kind of day-to-day existence. If this is so, I hope that you will want to risk emancipating yourself from a position of such self-devaluation—to consider a new vision of yourself.

I realize how we do have to stretch our imaginations of credulity sometimes. Hearing the words "be the best we can be" may sound impossible. However, when we make even a small beginning and find ourselves succeeding at anything, it is heady stuff. It suddenly dawns on us that "though much has passed, much still remains." In our "majority" years we can still do some wonderful things. We might, for example, potentially begin improving any one of the six preconditions to wellness that we have spoken of here.

A few years back I brought together eight people who in one way or another were discouraged with the direction of their lives. They had each been feeling a kind of ennui, a lack of enthusiasm about their daily activities and relationships. My experiences with similar groups made me aware that some of these forlorn people had come more out of curiosity than a real desire to participate. I asked them as a preliminary activity to try some activities to get their bodies and cardiovascular systems in relatively "excellent" shape.

This seemed about as foolish and inconceivable as they could possibly imagine, since for the most part, their self images were that of being unfit and unattractive. They were people ages twenty-four through sixty-one. Most had already heard a lot of advice about curing their despair that they felt had not been of great help. The new effort I suggested was to be quite different because they were going (after a medical check-up by a non-sedentary doctor) to do the seemingly *impossible*, become physically active where before they had been encouraged to passively consider solving their problems. In a relatively low-key way they were to become "athletes." A word that made them laugh until tears rolled down their cheeks as they stood together on the first day and looked each other over. "Misery loves company" they agreed among themselves.

I explained the wellness concept and told them that during our program each would have the opportunity of designing his own Therapeutic Life-Style. We would begin with our bodies since they would not visibly deceive us as to our real progress. We could have begun by doing almost anything physical to tone up muscles and arrive at aerobic fitness levels above those with which we started. However, I chose walking as the beginning since it got us outdoors and allowed even the most physically unfit to begin a wellness program. However, after this first activity, we were going to try running. To most of the group running seemed an impossible goal; however, it did have the element of challenge, and amusement.

By and large these people were used to failing, or sometimes never starting anything new in the first place. They already viewed themselves as having a wide variety of deficits: being too sedentary, uncoordinated, fat, having bad backs, being knock-kneed, having varicose veins, being too old (a favorite), too depressed, or simply a-shamed to appear on the street of their own town with "sweats" on. I assured them that their deficiencies were quite O.K. since the plan had been designed to capitalize on these very deficiencies. Furthermore, in following our program they would have, for the first time, a chance to measure the progress towards the goal called wellness. Step One was to become a "walker," Step Two, a "runner." This last declaration was greeted with continual amazement and a "Who's he kidding?" from one of the participants.

Twice a week we walked together, gradually learning to walk erect with our heads held proud. As the first weeks went by we met after each session to talk about how things were going in our lives, about friends with whom we had not been in contact, husbands or wives to whom we had not paid attention, kids from whom we might have been alienated, and our feelings of aloneness.

Gradually the pace and distance of walking increased from ambling a few blocks to faster walking for a mile or so. There were more and more times that we felt energized to stretch our horizons. If we were feeling particularly enthusiastic or playful we ran the distance from one telephone pole to the next.

I noticed new running shoes appeared, with self conscious apologies such as "Oh, my husband said I would ruin my arches." Many of our members imagined that the people behind the windows of the houses we passed must be laughing at this bunch of unathletic, "rag-tag" idiots. Yet each member of the group gained confidence. One day a fifty-nine year old woman in our group ran a block ahead of us and then ran back to the group beaming. Each week we continued picking up the pace, arms swinging, chatting like magpies.

Summer was approaching. Suddenly, one of the women appeared in running shorts and singlet. This was the woman who joined the group declaring that she "couldn't push herself away from the table, let alone from the refrigerator."

You might be asking yourself why these people even ventured to start such a far-out venture as this. I did myself sometimes. I guess the only answer was that most of them were at a particularly low point of their lives, a point where they wanted to gain more control of their existence. Over the months the group gradually divided itself into the "walk-run" division and the straight "running" contingent. By the end of six months each person in the group was walking or running regularly at least 2½ miles, 5 days or more a week. Some, including the fifty-nine year old woman, were talking of building their running strength further and began looking for an age group race to compete in.

I am not a promoter of running actually, although you sure can get hooked on it. I feel that there are a myriad of interesting activities that anyone, and I mean *anyone* at any age, can become involved in to get into relatively excellent physical shape. Certainly your sense of wellness increases proportionately as you do exercise over a sustained period. It seems clear to me that real exercise, far from making you tired, increases your energy source, until zingo, over a period of time your new activity becomes part of a life style which causes a feeling of well being.

"But, exercise is boring" you might be saying. Some of it is. That is why sometimes I start my exercising by riding a stationary bicycle for a half-hour each morning while watching the news on TV. But, mostly, if you are willing to conceive of exercise as a way of approaching your own "excellence" potential, it can become very pleasurable as well as necessary.

The part-time athlete, and I use the word here for anyone who aspires to train himself or herself towards physical excellence, finds that if wellness is possible in this area of his or her life, it is probably possible in others. The athlete also discovers that overeating, smoking, drugs, etc., are a hindrance to his total enjoyment in play. You begin exercising with some skepticism but as you experience your inner well-being it reinforces better expectations in other parts of your life.

Seeing yourself developing this first part of a therapeutic life-style and finding yourself challenged to do more, you begin to discover what you "can do" rather than what you "can't," and you keep pushing the boundaries outward. With this new philosophy the rest of your life opens to trying many new ways of expressing yourself. In learning to control your physical behavior in such a way that you are developing good habits for your body, you will achieve the health-oriented mind-set which allows you to stick to this one activity which will begin to raise your self-esteem as you do it. In my own case, I find the rest of my therapeutic life-style develops as I look at myself as a person capable of love, and having time now to activate those parts of my life that will continue to make me feel better. The things that I want to do are open to me, if I am open to them. Perhaps you too will find this to be true.

There are important mentors and other people in my past and present whom I would like to thank in the time left to me. I want them to know how important they have been. The same is true of people around me now. I can learn to be better and closer to the people in my current life structure. There is an excitement about this as I engage myself in a process of building and redirection. As Yogi Berra said so prophetically, the ball game "ain't over till it's over." Begin to remake your life into one you will dwell happily within.

I know a woman I will never forget. Her family had relegated her to a nursing home bed where it was expected she would live out her life. But she looked around her at the people on the ward where she was and she said, "I'm not going to die before my time." And she began to exercise her body in every way she could, after years of neglect and with a lot of grit and determination she got out of bed and gradually out of the nursing home. No one thought she could do it.

One of the things she found was a belief in herself. She also understood that what she had to do in part was to depend upon herself almost completely. One of the keys to dealing with loneliness is in developing this capacity to enjoy independent time with yourself. (This is a different, more productive kind of time than sitting passively watching actors acting out make-believe lives on the TV screen.) It is like becoming your own most trusted friend. That is why I believe that building up your own interests and separate ways of being creative are two of the most important assets to not feeling lonely. You have yourself, you have your special interests, and you learn that the confidence this generates in you will make it easier to be involved with other people. You are not dependent on them because you have your own resources, which complement their companionship. They benefit from your strength as well, so that the relationship becomes mutually reinforcing.

It is therapeutic for me to concentrate now on being an independent person who feels connected to his family, but who also remains individually involved in learning new skills and trying new things. For example, during my lifetime I have played the guitar, the violin, harmonica, and drums, all poorly. When I get to that part of my life where I will be forced to be somewhat sedentary I plan to take up learning to play a musical instrument "superbly." I am even so bold as to dream of playing in the local symphony orchestra. My dreams don't stop here by any means, I hope yours don't either. In a way, the mature part of your adult life is only the beginning. It is not a time to remain poised amidst starting blocks, saying "goodbye" to life before you say "hello."

I remember that when my kids were very small and we had been driving somewhere for a long while and getting tired, I would pull the car over to the side of the road and we would burst from the car doors and scoot around the car three times to get our energy back for the rest of the trip. Using the same analogy, maybe this is a good time to get up out of our rocking chair of boredom, run around it three times to prove to ourselves that we still have the breath.

Do you notice that you probably haven't thought about loneliness much in the last few minutes? We have been looking at actions rather than reactions which has allowed our minds to go exploring as opposed to looking regretfully at the limits we impose upon ourselves. I have tried to emphasize that there are no gimmick answers to all the aspects of loneliness. It is hard to convince yourself sometimes that you are more capable than you imagine. I know that for me finding inspiration through other people has always been more valuable than receiving instructions. That doesn't mean I don't hunger to learn. But sometimes facts don't help as much as trust in intuition. Knowing that older people statistically appear to be more capable of dealing with loneliness than younger ones may not be of particular value to me if I am filled with worry about being old and lonely.

What does seem exciting though, is discovery—like finding out how our daily actions become the source of our life theme—spelling out who we are in terms of who we allow ourselves to be. Time is important to me as is living fully because both are ways of merging successfully with death.

But you and I are alive now—the chances are that we have some solid time ahead of us. I enjoy considering that if we are going to leave an imprint on this earth we will need to take some further steps. And there is always this lovely and consoling poem by T. S. Eliot to strengthen our resolve:

> We shall not cease from exploration
> And the end of all exploring
> Will be to arrive where we started
> And know the place for the first time.

ELEVEN

GROWING from LONELINESS
(A summing up)

A Time Magazine (1979) story read in part:

. . . . . So ended last week the life of John Spenkelink, 30, a wiry drifter and habitual criminal after a frenzied week of final appeals . . . . Spenkelink was the first person involuntarily executed in the U.S. since 1967. In the final moments of his life, Spenkelink delivered a cryptic epitaph:
> MAN IS WHAT HE CHOOSES TO BE.
> HE CHOOSES THAT FOR HIMSELF.

When I am alone I sometimes come to that very deep place where I am able to be open to currents of feeling and thought with which I do not otherwise connect. John Spenkelink's words touch me in a way that is difficult to express because it is so personal. I see my own life in terms of his; in relation to choices I did or did not make. This is especially true in connection with the rhythms of my moving emotionally towards or away from people, and I think how often loneliness reflects these choices.

Hugh Prather mirrors my mind with his writing when he says in *Notes on Love and Courage* that:

In a lifetime I will lay eyes on thousands of human beings,

across rooms, on the streets, inside buildings. What will become
of it? Nothing. Absolutely nothing. Unless I change my attitude, they will remain a part of the dull background.

The word *choice* can be a painful one if you are depressed or lonely. The feeling so often is that you have run
out your string of options and there are no choices left, or if
there are, they must be painful ones at best. In desolate
times, one reaches the log-jam where discouragement, dis-
tortions, fear of failure, and problems of self-confidence
play such damaging roles. Such feelings give credence to
the idea that there is not really a special state of loneliness,
only self-devaluation.

On the positive side, becoming aware of lonely feelings
and admitting them is a point of beginning. In previous
chapters I have related some of my feelings about beginnings. Here we will be starting out among the same new/
old friends, *acceptance* and *attitude*, that are becoming
hallmarks of our exploration. We have come to a place
where I feel we must admit how much our *present attitude*
continues to affect our lonely feelings. Accepting this as
useful information may seem a dangerous leap into the
dark, because it means loneliness opens the possibility of
looking deeply into ourselves—to consider change when
change may seem so difficult.

One connector that might be used to bridge the gap
between lonely feelings and the actions to deal with them
is contained in the meaning of the single word, *CONNEC-
TION*. The issue of connection is the very heart of loneliness and forms the basis for un-loneliness. I propose that:

- Being lonely is simply being a person within a
  situation.
- The situation is an inability to make connections.
- The troubling area of connection is either some
  self-contained *inner* environmental problem such
  as a sense of alienation from the healthy self, or
  some *outer* environmental sense of disconnection
  from specific things or people.

● In both cases, loneliness is an *internal feeling of non-connectedness.*

Being "connected" or "unconnected" is something we all know something about. These two words seem to me to be tangible and commonly understood. Moreover, unconnectedness is a condition that is translatable into action terms.

I believe that *feelings will change when we take action,* and that often we can observably test these actions to see what the results will be. The fundamental benefit of action is that as we perceive ourselves being in control, we automatically diminish our susceptibility to loneliness or anxiety in any form, both phenomena of non-control.

Perhaps you view yourself now as being completely without any competency or redeeming features with which to handle your life. Perhaps you see yourself devoid of friends and at the bleakest end of the Loneliness Continuum. Perhaps it feels like the very best that you can manage right now is to exist. Perhaps staying in your position of loneliness (unconnectedness) is a choice you are making in the hope that someone will notice you. I accept where *you* are. However, I'm saying that for *me,* and I would hope for you, choosing to admit that we are lonely can become a springboard, if we let it. We can begin a chain of positive events into which the various factors that we have talked about throughout this book which might be fitted together, step by step, into some flexible, designed-by-you system for the management of lonely feelings. Regardless of where on the Continuum you are, I believe that some part of the system can become a "connector" but no such design will be effective without the desire for change.

Managing Loneliness is Managing Life

The element of *choice* is important in designing my own method for managing loneliness. It came out of some dissatisfaction with the way things were going for me some years ago. Dissatisfaction can be a powerful motivator and should be heeded. Over the years this self-management system has become such an ingrained part of my thinking that I really enjoy calling it my "philosophical/therapeutic life-style." Put in simple terms, it is a philosophy that accepts life as a series of opportunities and choices, some easy, some difficult. Within the time that I have available, my intention is to learn as much as I can, to be happy without hurting other people, treasure each ongoing moment, and not be afraid. Along the way I may blunder into some wrong-way passages; I already have. Still, I do the very best that I can to pick myself up and go on, knowing that life is never a stable process. One of the things I have learned along the way is not to be so afraid of failing, and to realize that it is through *acceptance* of the possibility of failure that all satisfying efforts are under-taken.

When I use the term "therapeutic life-style," I'm accept-ing that when I am honest I feel fine, when I am dishonest I feel lousy. It is therapeutic for me to recognize that the outcome of my strivings has value and that I learn and can grow from my mistakes, almost more than I can from my successes. Accepting this is a choice I make. It is part of the *self-management* package.

I have been attempting to demonstrate that loneliness, solitude, and aloneness describe basic human conditions that are of themselves nothing to fear. Our problem is with the *fear* of being alone, which includes the fear of not being in control. It is a fear that has been somewhat compounded by our living in a society that colludes in and sanctions alienation from our deepest feelings. This sense of aliena-tion conspires with fear to distort the character and mean-ing of our lonely feelings. And this brings me to my theme which is a simple one: unknowingly, we have allowed ourselves to be duped. Largely because of these three fac-tors, *a motif of which runs through people's experience of loneliness is criticism of the self.* It is no longer surprising to me that in my research I have found that people who live alone are not necessarily more lonely than people who do not. Mental outlook, rather than living situation, appears to be the single most important factor in finding fulfillment.

A common misperception that I often find being expressed is the notion that a single traumatic event can shape one's life forever. Certainly single events can have enormous impact, but I have come to believe that our general character is formed over a lifetime and is colored by the sequence of thousands of minute-by-minute events throughout the years. These are events that are continuing even now and that we can still largely learn to direct and control. Many people have trouble accepting this point of view and tend to give up because they don't see any way out of their present dilemmas but they give up too soon.

My friend, Toni Vallier, was like this. She was a woman who was preoccupied with remembering how beautiful she "used to be." Now, at age forty-five, she was feeling rusted out, lonely, and wondering out loud where the good times all had gone.

Typically, I felt, she had lost sight of what was keeping her lonely right now by focusing her attention upon how she had lost her attractiveness, and how this had made her lonely in the first place. So I told her that when she could learn to let go of her preoccupation with her former beauty, she might begin to find out how attractive she had become. Of course, this kind of advice seldom works, as I learned again when her reply was similar to Marleen's, "But what do you do when you are lonely?"

I remember telling her that I first began to think about *managing loneliness* after I had decided to come to grips with some critical aspects of myself:

— I was not totally happy with the way I was.
— A decision to make changes was in order.
— I would have to do this mostly alone.
— Without my continuing commitment,
  nothing would change.
— I would need to take a first step.

Of course, the ultimate problem is beginning the journey

to wellness. But in questioning what I wanted for myself, I recognized that I had already begun. I had a moral code. I had some idea of how I would like things to be. I'd been around a bit, seen some things, I told myself. I began to understand that the beginning steps at least were already within my grasp and my ability. I relaxed some and felt better. Over time, I continued to put ideas together. It's not loneliness so much that troubles you as distrust of yourself.

My first premise became: *By changing my perception of loneliness, I can change its impact upon me, therefore the outcome.* I have learned that real loneliness begins when I fail myself in some way, either by living with some kind of a lie or by being so involved in myself that I somehow fail other people as friend, helper, parent, lover. That is when intense loneliness pursues me and I find no peace. The *enemy* is within me when I live lies as is the *friend*, when I live honestly.

In its immediacy, loneliness is unsharable; there is a deep place within us that can never be touched or experienced by anyone else, and that is where we have to encounter ourselves. Our real problem (or pleasure) is in building a better relationship between the inner person, that essential core in which energy and truth lies, and the outer "doer" who acts and reacts in relation to others. If we utilize them effectively, lonely feelings can serve as a catalyst and guide.

Seeing things in this light, I believe, leads naturally to this second premise: As principal motivator of all our behaviors, *the loneliness experience can be utilized as a positively-charged avenue for personal growth.* Each experience of loneliness involves us in a confrontation with ourselves. The question becomes "How can we gain from this self-encounter?" I believe that we can do this by accepting the painful immediacy of our lonely inner experience as part of a valuable learning process that connects us with reality.

There will always be pain and sorrow in life, as well as joy. Risk and anxiety cannot be denied. During the most painful periods of my life I come to understand that I could not hide or avoid life. The way out was not to attempt to hold back from experiencing life but to experience more life. *The transition between loneliness and healing is to reach out and find others.* The movement often becomes self-reinforcing along two fronts almost simultaneously. As we develop ways to become more self-sufficient and comfortable during periods of aloneness, we can consequently be energized to improve our emotional commitment to other people who are important to me or who will become important.

My third premise is this: *Everything starts with awareness.* The one thing that we can never deny to ourselves is whether we feel badly or well. Feelings are real and we need to accept that they tell us something. When you have painful feeling, and you say to yourself, "I'm lonely," you have begun the process of reaction. In order to resolve guilt, or pain, or any other emotional response, the central issue must first be established. As Frederic Perls has ably pointed out, ". . . avoidance is the main characteristic of 'neurosis,' and its correct opposite is connection."

A friend of mine, Ken Rosenthal, puts it clearly: "In most cases the only problems which are insurmountable are those which are unstated, kept hidden, brooded about but unknown and therefore not amenable to being dealt with."

This brings us to the fourth premise: *The essential power to heal ourselves always comes from within. Our loneliness provides us with a doorway to reality through which we can focus our attention.*

A provocative statement attributed to Rainer Maria Rilke has proved useful to me many times over:"There is no place that does not see you — You must change your life."

My study of loneliness has helped me to understand that I should make no real demarcation between my daily acts and my spiritual life. In this way religion, for me, has become belief in affirmative action. It comes out of the conviction that no one can provide me with another life; I am immersed in this one. I don't believe that I can wait for something to happen. Some people wait too long and feel "ill." Others feel "ill" and wait too long. As for me, I agree with George Sheehan when he says, "From the moment you become a spectator, everything is downhill. It is a life that ends before the cheering and the shouting die."

The Life/Loneliness Management Plan

One of the special people I have counseled, Toni, made a beginning place of sorts, when she demanded of me, "Dick, what do you do when you are lonely?" I told her that I begin with what I know: bits of this or that picked from wherever, things that clearly have left an imprint upon me. I might begin, for example, by recalling this admonishment from an Ashleigh Brilliant cartoon.

ONE POSSIBLE REASON WHY THINGS AREN'T GOING ACCORDING TO PLAN IS THAT THERE NEVER WAS A PLAN.

For me, hoping for something better seldom brings results; keeping busy isn't enough. Moreover my loneliness is not going to be banished by sermons on "positive thinking." Insight into causes is only insight into causes; it is not change, or even planning for change. Thinking things out is a step, just as awareness is a beginning, but they are not enough; *skills and action must follow realization* in order to effect change.

Each of us creates our own special fulcrums. The Ashleigh Brilliant cartoon was one that worked for me. I have developed my own "plan," my own loneliness management system and endeavored to put it into practice. It has developed pretty much as follows and perhaps you may be able to utilize some of its aspects in confronting your own pain.

Consideration No. 1. Consider yourself an Instrument of Change — In doing this, I accept my responsibility to use my own personal attributes, my own resources, my own energy. My human-beingness is the instrument for improvement that I will be using. Consideration No. 1

concentrates on the inner self and on accepting that I will relate as a changed person with new vision to the real world. Here is where I say to myself, "At least I know what I don't want; now I'll begin to say to myself what I do want." It is the point where *awareness* translates into *action*. (I began by looking inward at the way that I perceived myself and then outward at the way I felt other people saw me. I did this as honestly as I could.)

When I talked with behavioral psychologist, B. F. Skinner about my project, he suggested that it would be important for me to emphasize that we are not going to change the inner conditions called "feeling," but that as we do change either the inner or outer environment that brought about our feelings in the first place, we will discover that those emotions also change.

Consideration No. 2. Resolve to do Something — I began by realizing that I had spent an awful lot of useless time looking backwards at my life, or feeling that because I had been lonely I was somehow deficient. I finally made a conscious choice to make active changes. I decided it was high time to regain control of my body, which had grown soft and overweight. Also, I needed to change the negative belief system which kept me worrying about things that I never really needed to obsess over in the first place. (When I first thought about a title for Consideration No. 2, I called it *"Support the Dream"* because I wanted to emphasize my impression that lonely people often unwisely give up striving for those higher aspirations that they had for themselves when they were feeling stronger and more connected.)

So, I began with a few new insights which built almost naturally into a resolve. Sometimes with me, any action is better than no action, and I felt buoyed up by having decided what I didn't like and what I hoped to do something about. I remember that just making that resolve, without worrying how I would bring it about, was a tremendous relief.

The old guard at the various alcoholic and drug rehabilitation centers around this country says:

"YOU'VE GOT TO DO MORE
THAN TALK THE TALK.
YOU'VE GOT TO BEGIN
TO WALK THE WALK."

As a way of taking that first small step (not for mankind, but for myself) I reverted to my need to try and reduce things to simple items. First, I made a poster and hung it over my shaving mirror where I could see it each new morning.

At the bottom of the poster, I drew a water scene with a boy riding through the waves on the back of a dolphin.

The dolphin symbolized the energy and excitement of life to me. Across the top of my poster I wrote in bold letters:

"UNDER NEW MANAGEMENT"

My sign was tangible proof that at least I understood the need for change. As I pondered my next moves, I couldn't help thinking how intimidated I had allowed myself to be at those earlier times when I had not understood the nature of my feelings. Loneliness was the prime example. Loneliness had been a misunderstood companion which I now wanted to learn to understand better. This would necessitate shucking off false pride and dishonesty while adding objectivity as a way of re-affirming myself as my own untapped resource. In short, I needed a more balanced assessment of Dick Price. If there was to be a Guru around here, I would have to be it. Even as a new Guru, I recognized that *distrust* in my own inner resources had kept me vulnerable to loneliness. There are times when we are so unaware of our needs that we cannot do what is required to gain fulfillment. As we come to assess our strengths as well as our weaknesses we need to distinguish where along the Loneliness Continuum we are. Asking ourselves how great the *distance* is between our goals and our perception of where we are now helps us establish a reality base from which to begin.

I have found that in examining what inner resources we have at hand, it is useful to distinguish between two of the gray areas responsible for our discontent. Are we in the predominantly *"Loneliness"* area, where whatever was lost is still in our minds? Or in the predominantly *"Emptiness"* area, where we have been unable over a period of time to achieve a stable concept of our own "good self?" It is too easy to say, "I'm both," and let it go at that. By using the self-management system progress can be made in either one of the two general areas, although there may be some overlapping.

Consideration No. 3. Make a Frank Self-Appraisal — (Strengths first, weaknesses second.) Sprinkle humor generously as needed to sustain objectivity. For me, it was much easier to do the "weaknesses" side of the ledger once I had filled the other side with reinforcing plusses. I believe it is over-weighting of our negative sides that makes loneliness so much more formidable than it needs to be.

(It isn't really necessary to be overly compulsive about all this. Some people hate lists, others don't have the energy, etc., etc. What's needed is to think about it comfortably, enjoying the leisure of spending some time with oneself.)

Each of us can build his or her positive and negative lists. We often do it in our heads anyway, but now at least we are doing it with some degree of order and balance. Somehow I find that as these details get pinned down and opened to scrutiny they seem less encompassing and intimidating. They become more "bite-size" and approachable. I have to agree with the philosophy of the character Glad, in the theatrical adaptation of Frances Hodgson Burnett's novel, *The Dawn of a Tomorrow,* when she points out:

There's a lot of things 'appens in this 'ere world: And I've seen abaht arf of 'em, I 'have. But there's one thing I ain't come across yet: that's a thing as was as bad as yer thort it was. There ain't nothin' as bad as that.

In my own case, just basking in the better aspects of self-evaluation generated a groundswell of other ideas. For example, I recalled and put to use the optimistic maxims of a favorite cousin of mine. The first one went something like this:

"When things seem darkest, remember this: Quite unknown to the general public is the strange coincidence that most things, either with or without a little shove, get better by themselves. Given half a chance, most things, in fact, are better by morning."

I found the second adage she presented to be doubly reassuring:

"The morning is wiser than the evening."

Carried along by the swiftly flowing enthusiasm of these new-found supports, my mind seemed receptive and open. I had to be careful not to close off my sensitivities to feel too secure. I needed, in fact, to allow myself to remain vulnerable if I were to experience my insights and life deeply.

I tried to look at myself as a camera might see me, without the layers of self-criticism that I might otherwise have heaped on my self-portrait but with the lens of truth. The beauty of a camera is that it does not judge you. I tried to maintain this same unbiased image of myself, so that I could be less dependent upon other peoples' opinions of me.

Sometimes when I'm not careful, my writing things out in order to clarify them becomes a way of avoiding putting thoughts into actions, but I was not going to allow this to happen this time. I made an honest list. It contained several traits that I did not admire in myself and which I felt explained why I sometimes had difficulty accepting myself and my talents.

I recognized that characteristically I had looked at some of the bad stuff first. But strangely, just generating the list was reclaiming control of events. Lists such as this have convinced me that, far from being "neurotic," *pain, anxiety, and a sense of guilt about these things is a healthy reaction, just as our lonely feelings are a testimony to the natural drives in all of us to interrelate successfully.*

I've been impressed with the number of lonely people who have been able to "diagnose" their own problems but felt that they could not mobilize their resources and gain a better feeling place. They know the problem, and even the potential solutions, but they see it as too difficult to begin the process. So I find it a fascinating thing, this word, "can't." For example, you might try a little experiment for yourselves. Whenever you tell yourself that you "can't" do something such as: "I can't go down to the park today because I know that they may not ask me to the barbeque and I'll feel uncomfortable," substitute the word, "won't" and see what happens. See if it changes or illuminates your feelings. For me, "won't" is a word that comes closer to my accepting the responsibility for my actions or non-actions.

So much depends upon *attitude*. We don't just have good ideas on demand, we attain them through trial and error. In terms of loneliness, I feel not trying can be the greatest hazard we face because it is a stagnating condition, a condition which offers no hope for change.

Loneliness cannot be pushed aside. Instead, it needs our attention, and *when we have* finally *accepted* its presence, it may have already begun to leave us.

Consideration No. 4. Develop a New Plan to Get Where You Want To Go — To do this, take the information that you collect about yourself and your situation and begin to make a plan, even a foolish one, about changing it. Try to remain open to new ideas by letting go of any old unsuccessful goals and old failures of plans that are still rumbling around in your mind. Let the past go, try to find fresh ideas more relevant to current need, then create a plan for change. If you start with understanding more about your inner self, you can end with real goals for new activities to carry out.

Each of us eventually will act in our own way. A lot of people try the cocktail lounge or the bar scene as a way to meet other people and find intimacy, but end up feeling more alone. Others join church groups, Parents Without Partners, or volunteer to help out in community activities. Some change jobs, take up bowling, etc., and then find that the new situations satisfies their need to regain a sense of participation and belonging. It is a beginning for them. Maybe such ideas can be a beginning for you.

In a way, it takes putting one foot in front of the other, with no apologies needed for previous failures. My hope is that this process will accelerate the elimination of "stock answers," such as, "But I tried that a year ago, and it didn't work," or the self-fulfilling clincher, "I wouldn't be here if something wasn't wrong with me." Lonely people often tenaciously hold on to these stock answers and get blocked in their own self fulfilling, damaging prophesies.

One of the lonely of whom we've spoken, Marleen, kept saying that the only way she could live was through someone else; she kept wondering how she could find herself. I am reminded of the questions that I offered her at that time. They were the same questions I have asked many other lonely people, and her answers were similar to theirs.

"In all of this terrible and hopeless experience of loneliness that you have been in, is there anything, anything at all, that has been good about it or which is useful to you now?" Her first reply was "nothing." "Anything at all that you have learned about yourself as a result of this experience that could be useful to you now?" "No."

"Marleen, is everything black in this experience? *Isn't there anything you've learned?*"

"No, well, unless it's. . . ." and suddenly, a little chink appears in the defensive armor of the lonely who won't acknowledge anything of value from this suffering.

My experience has been that once you allow yourself the risk of considering that the distressing thing that now has a hold upon you just might have some redeeming feature, might, by some wild stretch of the imagination, become a valuable tool, your whole perception of it changes; feelings alter, faces light up. *Loneliness can never be seen in a purely negative light again.* Once people begin to explore their painful experiences we can change the way we deal with reality. We can begin doing it more effectively, so that we feel better and better about ourselves. (Doing this in little steps doesn't mean we're *little* people, and the imaginary dragons out to slay us often reside in our very large imaginations.)

Like many of us, Marleen had trouble staying focused on present moments of her life. She lingered in her sense of failure as though the present did not exist.

My thoughts go back to how she tried to read my face as though it would contain the message she searched so hard to find. I remember saying:

"Marleen, you tell me you are feeling lonely. I hear you telling me again in great detail about your feelings. You speak of frustration and lack of confidence, even despair, an imprisoned bird held captive by invisible bars."

"You are surprised that I stop you before you have finished. You wonder, 'Doesn't he care? Am I boring him'?"

"Oh no, you've convinced me quite well that you are lonely and it hurts. You are stuck."

"You are surprised again when I say, 'O.K., I hear you, but *what are you doing*'?"

"'I'm feeling lousy,' you answer, wondering why this wasn't obvious to me. But I persist, not because I don't care, but because I do."

"My perception of you is that you are equating *feelings* with *doing.* However, I'm asking you about actual behavior you are engaged in now. What did you do yesterday, today and so on? I am asking the questions because I feel that your continued engagement with your lonely feelings, rather than the actions that brought them about is what is keeping you stuck. Involvement with your *feelings* often precludes involvement with *other people,* and you've been telling me how lonely you are for companionship." In China, there are two characters in the symbol representing the word "crisis." One is the symbol for danger, meaning you have to deal with this, and the other is the symbol for opportunity. The crisis of loneliness creates opportunity to take self-responsibility. I say to Marleen and other "People of the Mirror" that *my own way of conceptualizing the loneliness void is not "emptiness," but uncreated potential waiting to be used.*

Consideration No. 5. Take Charge of Making Things Happen — (Appreciate what you have done thus far.) Then move beyond data collection, making a plan and organizing things, to acting on your ideas. Anxiety often goes down as you regain control. You are no longer a victim of circumstance. I often find it helpful in becoming unlonely (connected) to do something for someone else, and to do it with whatever caring and love is in me. What I do must be genuine. Perhaps it will only be to write a letter or make a phone call, saying something I wanted to communicate but had not managed to say before. When I give something of myself to someone else, something good always seems to come back, especially when I give it without expecting any return. I think of something my wife wrote to me one time, while I was away and loneliness was on her mind.

"... I jotted down some notes on what Barry Kaufman said on the radio last night—my sentiments exactly. 'Happiness is listening to your own voice, without conforming. Beliefs can make us unhappy, change the belief and the whole world changes.' It occurred to me that I would be lonely when you were away at times. I have not been, which is neither good or bad. The point is, I said I would be lonely. I said it to myself Friday night, when I woke up and I said it to Dot when I left her to come home Saturday. I love you and will be glad when you too, are home."

CONSIDERATION No. 6. Reconstruction of a Sense of

Self Must Be Nourished By a New Kind of Communication
With Other People — Contained within our new perception of loneliness as a teacher, within our new knowledge
that our universal motivating drive is to be unlonely, is a
positive seeking response which leads us continually towards experiences of each moment's enrichment of our
lives. As my friend, Shaun McNiff, wrote in a recent note to
me:

> ". . . I realize that I have always seen the answer for
> me in having communion with each moment—as an
> artist I commit myself to the 'sacrament' of com-
> munion by giving sensible form to those felt relation-
> ships—it is a process of communion with the
> moment, no matter what it may be. . ."

If, as Shaun says, "The sacrament of communion" at
each moment gives sensible form to felt relations, then I
think we have to keep asking ourselves some basic questions: How long has it been since I paid full attention to
someone else's need? When did I last really listen to some
other person telling me his or her problems, successes,
feelings? What attention do I give to my peripheral relationships, for instance, the woman at the drug center? Did I
simply hand the money over to the arm extended from an
unseen torso, without seeing the face? Did I try to feel her
special presence or leave without feeling any connectedness? Are my concerns so important to me, is my inner
dialogue so fascinating to me, is my separateness so precious to me that I cannot or will not reach out and share my
humanness with others?

I think each of us knows more or less what keeps us
lonely. Also, we generally realize that there are options
and actions we could take to relieve our distress when we
are lonely. Lonely people can reach out to others. Just look
in the phone book or newspaper, there are social groups,
singles groups, groups for divorced persons, groups for
bereaved persons, church groups, poetry groups, bowling
groups, and evening groups. There are literally hundreds

of activities going on each day. Yesterday in the paper there were ads for new job openings, educational opportunities, ski trips, music courses, plays, pleas for volunteers, big brothers and sisters, concerts, personal growth groups, ad infinitum. Consider the hundreds of thousands of people who gather to run together each weekend, or swim at the Y.M.C.A. or take nature walks. It becomes a question of *when and how involved* we will *allow* ourselves to be.

Consideration No. 6. Make a Commitment to Follow Through — I generally subscribe to the premise, "I can if I want to." This is one of the times when assertiveness may be necessary. No outside force is keeping us lonely, so the impetus is within our control. Managing loneliness, and life in general, is largely a matter of *acceptance* and *practice.*

I cannot help but be impressed by the relationship between the inability to take effective action and low self-esteem. So many of the people whom I interviewed in my practice or for this book wanted to develop special interests and gratifying competencies of their own but, for one reason or another had not achieved these goals during their past lives. This lack of hobbies or outside interests made it difficult for them to feel self-contained and able to entertain themselves in times of stress such as after a relationship had broken up, or they were alone. Once their inertia ended and they found the energy to look into some special interest, whether it was collecting fossils, playing cards, making music, creating ceramic bowls, etc., they then found something in the present to "turn on" to and something in the future to continue to develop and anticipate. They became connected to something tangible which was clearly an expression of themselves. The more they were able to enjoy their new found creativity, the more they were able to share this with others. Time, which had hung so heavily on their hands, now moved more swiftly and held greater promise. Self-sufficiency and loneliness do not go hand in hand.

I want to be very clear about the process of "self-help." There are many times in my life when any formal system for managing intense problems seems impossible and unnatural. At these times, I stop the whole intellectual inner-processing business that we have been outlining here and simply try to relax and become totally unattached from "head trips," rationality, and planning. Whatever else is open to me—taking a walk or a run through the country-side, calling up a friend to go out to lunch, or just taking a drive to some new place becomes an interim release from nervous tension. It is important here to emphasize that nothing so orderly as a list, or management system, or anyone else's ideal solution, has value if the timing is wrong, or the method doesn't make sense to you. It can even become counterproductive if you don't believe in it. My reason for presenting some of what works for me is to point out that there are some options which may be of help in lonely periods.

There is so much more I want to say. I began this project knowing that there were certain aspects of loneliness about which I had my own theories. There still are. The inevitable old questions linger, "What do you hope will happen if you write about this?" "So what?" "Who cares?" These are unanswerable questions. I decided to act on an adage I have faith in: "Start with what you believe and go with that." The moment always comes when we must bring this understanding to active life. This book is, for me, that moment.

I think of the old tortoise shell hand mirror that hangs in the entry hall of a house on Galiano Island. It lost its reflective glass face some time ago, and now, if you hold it up and look straight out through the open frame, you can see in the distance how the long curving edge of the Pacific Ocean incisively meets the sky. Or, you can just hold it up, as I have also done, and think how its rounded frame represents the circle of your life, which you fill in with whatever colors and definition *you alone* choose.

This has been my way of seeing loneliness. Your own way will be even more important. We both need to respect that.

Books Of Particular Value

Buscaglia, Leo, *Love*, New York: Fawcett Crest Books, 1972
As the cover says, "A Warm and wonderful book, about the largest experience in life." I feel that the connection between the fear of love, or the fear of expressing love, and the fear of loneliness and the way loneliness is expressed, is of paramount importance to almost anyone who feels frightened and alone. This is a tender and inspiring book, which made me re-examine the way that I communicate with other people. It just left me smiling.

Friedman, Meyer, and Roy H. Rosenman, *Type A Behavior and Your Heart*, New York: Fawcett Crest, Paper, 1976.
I think every "busy man" could benefit from reading this book. Although this is a study of heart attack victims, it is also a fascinating look at the behavior patterns that lead many men, and increasing numbers of women, towards the great American "hurry sickness" that eventually kills. It is a study of men particularly who continue to neglect their physical and emotional health, and perhaps their families, in the process of over-striving to achieve success. The findings of this book may startle you, and give you a sense of direction towards seeking some peace within yourself. I found it a valuable adjunct in the study of loneliness.

Glasser, William, *Positive Addiction*, New York: Harper and Row, 1976.

I appreciate the straightforward, no-nonsense approach that the author of *Reality Therapy* brings to "self-help" management techniques, as well as to personal growth. If I were not a runner, this book would still intrigue me, because it illustrates so well how we might each find something that really excites us which then becomes a rewarding, ongoing involvement.

Gordon, Suzanne, *Lonely In America*, New York: Simon and Schuster, 1976.
A comprehensive overview of the social and psychological forces which shape the American experience of loneliness. I appreciate the chapters on "the loneliness business"—encounter groups, therapists, gurus, who may exploit the lonely. A solid portrait of what it is like to be lonely in our country, and a look at how people are dealing with it.

Howard, J. A., *The Flesh-Colored Cage*, New York: Hawthorn Books, 1975.
A sensitive look at woman's/man's essential aloneness and the resultant effect upon his/her attitudes and behavior.

Kostrubala, Thaddeus, *The Joy of Running*, Philadelphia—New York: J. B. Lippincott, 1976.
You can forget the running if it turns you off, but you won't forget this true story of a psychiatrist who had allowed his mind and body to run down until forced to take a new action.

Lair, Jess, "I Ain't Much Baby—But I'm All I've Got," Greenwich, Conn.: Fawcett Crest Books, 1972.
A book of faith and hope. My impression is that just about everything contained in this book is useful to someone who is feeling lonely and in low spirits. I strongly recommend it as a "first reader" to all of Jess

Lair's other books. Each book seems to grow out of the other, and I feel each has great inspirational and practical value. When I first got hooked into reading Jess's books, the "hip" style seemed a bit much, but now it feels very genuine to me.

Several years ago I recommended this book to a woman friend, and she has actually carried it in her handbag ever since. She saw it as inspirational and it gave her a sense of confidence, because what it said was, "Look, your experience was much more normal than you thought, you're not really so way out bad to feel this way. Join the club. And I felt that way, too, and I'll tell you a little bit about it when you read my story," which Jess does very beautifully and she feels in touch with him. She feels like writing to him; some day she'd like to call him up. She's adopted a friend if you will, so the book has value for her. And it's partly in the way that he was able to write it, with a humanness that makes her think: "Here's a guy who's been somewhere I've been. He's known pain like I'm knowing pain, and he's worked his way through it, and he's a bright guy and he sounds like fun and I respect him. So I'll look at his work and try to emulate that part of it that I can." And that's what she's doing.

His main theme is that you've got to be able to tell people what you're feeling deep down in your heart, because if you can do that with them, they're going to turn around and be able to do it with you. That's how you're going to be able to get all those nice warm fuzzies and all those things that you want. He's not dealing so much with loneliness as he is with love— not getting enough love, which is basically very much related.

Lazarus, Arnold, and Allen Fay, *I Can If I Want To*, New York: William Morrow & Co., 1975.

There is possibly a tug in many of us to write the perfect "How To" book, that doesn't mislead, promise

too much, or take away from the reader's own capacity
to formulate satisfactory answers. I think the authors
achieved this goal quite well by presenting a step-by-
step problem solving methodology which makes
sense. This book highlights the importance of assertiveness in personal relationships, and points up that
the locus of control is in ourselves. I believe it can be
used as a guide to begin reassessing where you are
now and how to take charge.

Lynch, James T., *The Broken Heart—the Medical Consequences of Loneliness*, New York: Basic Books, 1977.
    An intriguing study of the relationship between emo-
tional and physical health. A testimony to the effects
of loneliness and loneliness-prone behavior in our
society. Packed with provocative examples of the
consequences of remaining lonely, plus some useful
ideas about what to do about it.

Moustakas, Clark E., *Loneliness*, New York: Prentice-Hall,
1961.
    Start with this one. This is an absorbing book by one
of the pioneers in the study of loneliness. I heartily
suggest that you will find something of value in each
of his books. Clark Moustakas presents a personal and
penetrating perspective into his own loneliness and
makes a forceful case for utilizing your loneliness
experience as a key to a deeper insight into yourself.
He views the movement from loneliness to an appreciation of solitude and the self.
    I have personally found Clark Moustakas to be a
beautiful person, as well as teacher, with a deep
understanding and empathy for human suffering, as
well as joy. I feel privileged to have studied with him
for a short while. During this time I found his own
deep spirituality expressed in the authentic way he
interacts with people.
    Just reading each of his many books on loneliness

has been a fascinating education in personal deve-lopment. He has gone into far greater detail through-out his books that I have to delineate and examine the interrelationship between Loneliness, Aloneness, Solitude, and Isolation.

Nouwen, Henry J. M., *Reaching Out*, New York: Doubleday and Co., Inc., 1975.
A spiritually inspiring book which examines three movements of the spiritual life: the movement from loneliness to solitude (our relationship to ourselves); the movement from hostility to hospitality (our rela-tionship to others); and the final, most important movement, from illusion to prayer (our relationship to God). I enjoyed the first half of this book particular-ly, in that it represented an insight into the connec-tion between our finding self-renewal in ourselves and the movement towards acceptance of solitude as a way of personal fulfillment.

Riesman, David, Nathan Glazer, and Reuel Denney, The Lonely Crowd, New Haven, Conn.: Yale University Press, 1961.
A fascinating and useful study of loneliness and the changing American character. An excellent classic resource to begin with and then to build upon in terms of a continuing focus on psychological/sociological aspects of loneliness.

Sarton, May, *Journal of Solitude*, New York: W. W. Norton and C., 1973.
May Sarton speaks of her own struggles and pleasures as a woman living generally alone. Each of her books appears to deal with being single, but still remaining involved and energized by other people, as well as by herself.

Schneidman, E. S., and M. J. Ortega, *Aspects of Depres-*

sion, Little, Brown and Co., 1969.
A very concise and fascinating book which I believe is useful in considering the relationship of loneliness to depression.

Schultz, Toni, *Bitter Sweet*, New York: Penguin Books, 1976.
A real sleeper! This is one of the most useful books that I have read on this subject. I believe that it will appeal to everyone who is lonely, but especially to women. It is written from a frank, provocative and somewhat feminist point of view. I found it to be a particularly honest and useful guidebook for anyone who felt "put down," "left out," or just plain "lousy." I felt that there were some excellent resources at the end of this book. (Note that the authors of many of these books also offer useful resources and reading suggestions.)

Sheehy, Gail, *Passages*, New York: E. P. Dutton and Co., 1974.
A national best seller and a must, I feel, for anyone who does not as yet believe that loneliness, fear of loss, separation anxiety, and other such life crises are a natural part of each of our lives. This book attempts to put the natural stages of growth and development into useful and understandable terms.

Tanner, Ira J., *Loneliness: The Fear of Love*, New York: Harper and Row, 1973.
Using the special language of Transactional Analysis this book emphasizes the important connections between not being able to give and/or receive love, and the fear of reaching out and expressing feelings. I believe that the proposition that it is fear which tends to keep us lonely is well taken, and needs to be considered by anyone who is feeling troubled that way.

Watts, Allen, *Cloud-Hidden, Whereabouts Unknown*, New York: Pantheon Books, 1968.

I really gain inspiration and pleasure from most of Allen Watt's writing. Of special value to me is the emphasis upon Eastern philosophy and ways of living within the balance of nature. I find Allen Watts both amusing and original. It is difficult to come away from the reading of his books without feeling how idiotic it is to rush about looking for happiness as though we could buy it, squeeze it out of something, or gain it through some advance in our technological culture. Watts connects us up with the thoughtful, appreciative part of our inner life, and the flowing Tao of nature itself. (I would suggest that between Allen Watts, Clark Moustakas and Jess Lair alone there are many productive weeks of reading ahead, plus the numerous allied readings that each author might suggest.)

Weiss, Robert S., *Loneliness—the Experience of Emotional and Social Isolation*, Cambridge, Mass.: The M.I.T. Press, 1973.

A thoughtful and factual breakdown of loneliness into two general categories. The best part of this book for me was contained in the informative discussion about organized groups such as Parents Without Partners, etc., who finds them the most helpful, and why. A good book for anyone who is trying to become socially re-connected after a separation. I find it a valuable reference work for older people who either live alone or are feeling confined and socially restricted.

Additional Reading:

Fromm-Reichmann, Frieda, "*Loneliness*" Psychiatry, February, 1959.

The classic in-depth look at the psychological aspects

of loneliness. I believe this is one of the best analyses of the phenomenon available. (Most libraries allow photo-copies to be made of articles such as this.)

Then there are books that touch the soul when we are lonely and needing something poignant and beautiful. For me, these are the quiet books that reflect upon our simple connections to nature, the loneliness, and to the love of someone else. I find that I often pick up these when I feel thoughtful, or bored, or lonely, and through them I often come away refreshed. My list of these books includes:

Kellog, Marjorie, *Like the Lion's Tooth*, New York: Farrar, Strauss, and Giroux, 1972.

Kotzwinkle, William, *Swimmer in the Secret Sea*, New York: Avon Books, 1975.

Kunhartdt, Philip B., Jr., *My Fathers House*, New York: Random House, 1958.

Merrick, Hugh, *The White Spider*, London: Rupert Hart-Davis, Ltd., 1959.

You might reasonably ask what these books have to do as resource books on the subject of loneliness. I believe that each of them touches upon the basic nature of life, which so often is pain overcome and joy experienced. I feel that certain aspects of each of these books serves both as a model and as an inspiration for learning to live through adversity. I think we learn to find strengths in what first appeared as weaknesses, and we find beauty and empathy and love where before we had overlooked them.

One final suggestion: for a much more detailed bibliography of books and articles on Loneliness, you might wish to write to:

Journal Supplement Abstract Service
American Psychological Association
1200 Seventeenth St., N.W.
Washington, D.C., 20036
Request: Document MS 1682—Loneliness
   (Ask for updated material)

Chapter Notes

CHAPTER TWO
Thomas Wolfe, *Look Homeward Angel* (New York: Grosset and Dunlop, 1929), p. 37.

CHAPTER THREE
Quotation from a speech by George A. Sheehan made at the *Boston Marathon Sports/Medicine Running Clinic*, Boston, April, 1979.

CHAPTER FOUR
Robert S. Weiss, *Loneliness—The Experience of Emotional and Social Isolation*, (Cambridge: The MIT Press, 1973).

Suzanne Gordon, *Lonely in America*, (New York: Simon and Schuster, 1976), p. 15.

William Glasser, *The Identity Society*, (New York: Harper and Row, 1975), p. 2.

Special Singles Section excerpt: Classified ad taken from *Steppin' Out*, Los Angeles: weekly special interest newspaper, (August, 1978).

Ibid.

James Weldon Johnson, *God's Trombones*, (New York: Viking Press, 1955) p. 17.

Stan Steiner, *The Vanishing White Man*, (New York: Harper and Row, 1976) p. 122.

CHAPTER FIVE
This quotation from Meister Eckhardt, presented to a group of runners attending *The Runners Expo-Sports/Medicine Clinic*, Boston, 1979, by George Sheehan.

Mirror, Mirror, quotation from a taped interview with Phyllis Lowry-Bell, Philadelphia, 1978.

For a more detailed study of each of these five words as they apply to loneliness, read Clark E. Moustakas' *Loneliness,* (New Jersey: Prentice-Hall, 1961), *Loneliness and Love,* (New Jersey: Prentice-Hall, 1972).

CHAPTER SIX

Clark Moustakas has written extensively in regard to loneliness anxiety. Refer to *Loneliness,* New York: Prentice-Hall, Inc., 1972).

Robert S. Weiss, *Loneliness—The Experience of Emotional and Social Isolation,* (Cambridge: The MIT Press, 1973). Definitions explained in greater detail in this work include references to "emotional isolation" and "social isolation," issues of "chronic" and "transient" loneliness, as well as "situational" and "characterological" theories of loneliness.

Reference to feeling forsaken taken from the Gospel according to St. Matthew, Chapter 27, Verse 26, *HOLY BIBLE—Revised Standard Version,* (Dallas: The Melton Book Co., 1952) p. 784.

Robert Benvenuto, *Loneliness and Creative Expression.* Unpublished master's paper (Cambridge: Lesley College Graduate School, Expression Therapies Department, 1979) p. 7.

Paulo Knill, *Expressive Therapies and Education.* Unpublished Ph.D. thesis, (Cincinnati: Union Graduate School, 1978).

George Sheehan, *Running and Being,* (New York: Simon and Schuster, 1978) p. 147.

Although Sigmund Freud may have intended to speak of the phenomenon of loneliness by implication in his extensive writings, my only knowledge of any specific references to the topic is found in one essay, "The Uncanny," printed in *The Complete Works of Sigmund Freud*, Vol. 17. (London: Hogarth, 1955).

Pamela Staffier, *The Philosophical Implications of Freud's Psychology*. Unpublished Ph.D. dissertation, (Cincinnati: Union Graduate School, 1979) p. 1.

Claire Weekes, *Agoraphobia*, (New York: Hawthorn Books, Inc., 1976) p. 48.

I first heard this quotation used by Michael Kahn, one of the leaders in a training workshop at the National Training Laboratory, Bethel, Maine, 1972.

Henry D. Witzleben, *On Loneliness*, Psychiatry 21 (1958), p. 37-43.

Aaron T. Beck and Jeffery E. Young, *College Blues*, Psychology Today (September 1978).

Terri Schultz, *Bitter Sweet*, (New York: Penguin Books, 1976), p. 13

Aaron T. Beck and Jeffery E. Young, *College Blues*, Psychology Today (September 1978).

A term described by Clark E. Moustakas during a workshop on Loneliness, (Bangor, Maine, 1978). Also used (along with "chronic loneliness") by psychotherapists and counselors in describing loneliness as an "illness."

Aaron T. Beck and Jeffery E. Young, *College Blues*, Psychology Today (September 1978).

Discussed by Clark E. Moustakas in a workshop on *Loneliness*, Bangor, Maine, 1973).

Robert S. Weiss, *Loneliness—The Experience of Emotional and Social Isolation*, (Cambridge: The MIT Press, 1973).

Ibid.

Regarding the topic of *Perception:* I believe that care-fully observing psychotherapists and counselors, etc. will often see in their clients' actions, patterns of behavior which they direct towards attempting to control their perception of how things are. William Glasser and William T. Powers are among a few re-searchers I am aware of who are also investigating aspects of personal behavior as a controller of percep-tions. William T. Powers has produced a book on this subject, *Behavior: The Control of Perception,* Chica-go, Aldine Publishing Company, (1973)—I have been influenced by some of their findings in my own form-ulation about perception.

CHAPTER SEVEN

Margaret Mead, *Coming of Age in Samoa,* (New York: Morrow Quill, 1961).

Margaret Mary Wood, *Paths of Loneliness,* (New York: Columbia University Press, 1953). Quotation from the unpublished master's thesis of Robert Davis, *Some Men of the Merchant Marine,* (New York: Facul-ty of Political Science, Columbia University, 1907) p. 165.

CHAPTER EIGHT

Hugh Prather, *Notes on Love and Courage,* (New York: Doubleday and Co., 1977).

Frederic S. Perls, *Ego Hunger and Aggression,* (New York: Random House, 1969) p. 189.

Kenneth Rosenthal, *INWARD BOUND—A Psycho-logical Guidebook for Men,* unpublished Ph.D. thesis (Cincinnati: Union Graduate School, 1977) p. 119.

George A. Sheehan, *Running and Being,* (New York: Simon and Schuster, 1978) p. 61.

Ashleigh Brilliant, "Pot Shots #571." This quotation published in *Precision Nirvana,* by Deane H. Shapiro,

Jr., (New Jersey: Prentice-Hall, Inc. 1978) p. 77.

Reference to *feelings* made by B. F. Skinner during a taped interview with me (Cambridge: 1978).

I first heard this *Walk the Walk* quotation used in an interview with members of the staff of "735," a drug rehabilitation program located in Wakefield, MA (1972).

Reference to the symbols for the word *crisis:* Dean H. Shapiro referred to the two characters of this word in a workshop sponsored by the Institute for Human Behavior, (New York City, 1979).

Bibliography

Beck, Aaron T. & Young, Jeffery E., *College Blues*, Psychology Today, September 1978.

Benvenuto, Robert, *Loneliness and Creative Expression*, unpublished Master's paper (Cambridge: Lesley College Graduate School, Expressive Therapies Department, 1979).

Freud, Sigmund, *The Complete Works of Sigmund Freud*, (London, Hogarth, 1955).

Glasser, William, *The Identity Society*, (New York: Harper and Row, 1975).

Gordon, Suzanne, *Lonely In America*, (New York: Simon and Schuster, 1976).

HOLY BIBLE—Revised Standard Version, (Dallas: The Melton Book Company, 1952).

Johnson, James Welton, *The Creation*, (New York: Viking Press, 1955).

Knill, Paulo, *Expressive Therapies and Education*, unpublished Ph.D. thesis, (Cincinnati: Union Graduate School, 1978).

Mead, Margaret, *Coming of Age in Samoa*, (New York: Morrow Quill, 1961).

Montagu, Ashley, *The Elephant Man*, (New York: E. P. Dutton, 1979).

Moustakas, Clark E., *Loneliness*, (New Jersey: Prentice-Hall, Inc., 1961).

Moustakas, Clark E., *Loneliness and Love*, (New York: Prentice-Hall, Inc., 1972).

Perls, Frederic S., *Ego Hunger and Aggression*, (New York: Random House, 1969).

Powers, William T., *Behavior: The Control of Perception*, (Chicago: Aldine Publishing Company, 1973).

Prather, Hugh, *Notes on Love and Courage*, (New York: Doubleday and Co., 1977).

Reichmann, Freida-Fromm, *Principles of Intensive Psychotherapy*, (Chicago: University of Chicago Press, 1950).

Reichmann, Freida-Fromm, *Loneliness*, Psychiatry, (February, 1959).

Shapiro, Deane H. Jr., *Precision Nirvana*, (New Jersey: Prentice-Hall, Inc., 1978).

Sheehan, George A., *Running and Being*, (New York: Simon and Schuster, 1978).

Shultz, Terri, *Bitter Sweet*, (New York: Penguin Books, 1976).

Staffier, Pamela, *The Philosophical Implications of Freud's Psychology*, unpublished Ph.D. dissertation, (Cincinnati: Union Graduate School, 1979).

Steiner, Stan, *The Vanishing White Man*, (New York; Harper and Row, 1976).

Webster's New Collegiate Dictionary, (Springfield: G. and C. Merriam Company, 1977).

Weeks, Claire, *Agoraphobia*, (New York: Hawthorn Books, Inc., 1976).

Weigert, Edith, *The Courage To Love*, (New London: Yale University Press, 1970).

Weiss, Robert S., *Loneliness—The Experience of Emotional and Social Isolation*, (Cambridge: The MIT Press, 1973).

Witzleben, Henry D., *On Loneliness*, Psychiatry, 21, (1958).

Wolfe, Thomas, *Look Homeward Angel*, (New York: Grosset and Dunlap, 1929).

Wood, Margaret Mary, *Paths of Loneliness*, (New York: Columbia University Press, 1953).